FLIP, SLITHER, & BANG
JAPANESE SOUND AND ACTION WORDS

FLIP, SLITHER, & BANG

Japanese Sound and Action Words

Hiroko Fukuda

translated by
Tom Gally

Kodansha International
Tokyo • New York • London

Distributed in the United States by Kodansha America, Inc. 114
Fifth Avenue, New York, N.Y. 10011, and in the United Kingdom
and continental Europe by Kodansha Europe Ltd., Gillingham
House, 38-44 Gillingham Street, London SW1V 1HU. Published
by Kodansha International Ltd., 17-14 Otowa 1-chome, Bunkyo-
ku, Tokyo 112, and Kodansha America, Inc.

93 94 95 10 9 8 7 6 5 4 3 2 1

ISBN 4-7700-1684-0

Contents

Preface

Japanese is difficult.

Or at least that's what some people say. But is it really so? I myself believe that Japanese is fun. And one aspect of the Japanese language that is the most fun of all is the topic of this book: onomatopoeia and mimesis.* The sound and action words of Japanese give the language its spice, its flavor. They bring life to what otherwise might be dull and bland, and they make your spoken Japanese more natural and expressive.

This book is a brief introduction to onomatopoeia and mimesis in Japanese through real-life conversations and examples. While presenting some of the most common sound and action words, I've added several other features to make the book even more useful.

The language in the book is natural spoken Japanese. Many people who study outside of Japan get a rude awakening when they first visit: they don't understand what anyone is saying. The reason is that the language they've learned from textbooks is stiff and unnatural, often unlike what is heard in everyday life. As a countermeasure of sorts, the conversations and examples given here are all in an informal spoken style, with a balance between women's and men's language. When you read this book, I hope you will feel as though you're having a nice friendly chat in Japanese, the way it would be done if you were talking to an actual person.

The topics show the real Japan. Contrary to popular belief, few Japanese have much to do with geisha, trade negotiations, or Mt. Fuji during their daily lives. The subject matter taken up in this book show what people actually talk about at home, at work, and at play.

Each of the main vocabulary items is marked G, N, or B (Good, Neutral, or Bad, to show if its sense if positive, neutral, or negative). After all, nothing is more embarrassing than to use a word that has the right meaning but the wrong connotation.

Brief notes provide information on cultural background. Every language is an essential part of the culture of the people who speak it, a window on the country's history and ways of thinking. That's why every language is different and difficult and fascinating. Learning another language is worthwhile because it gives you a link to other people, both as a vehicle for sharing ideas and as a practical tool for everyday life. But to attain a mastery of a language, you need more than grammar and vocabulary, so I've scattered notes throughout this book to provide some basic information about Japanese life and customs.

Typical Japanese names are used in the examples. It's hard to remember unfamiliar names in a foreign language. To help you out in this regard, I've made a point of using the ten most common surnames and a variety of common given names.

Illustrations show the settings of each conversation. If you've never visited Japan, these drawings should help you visualize the speakers and their surroundings.

You can read the book in any order. Some people always start on the first page of a book and read straight through to the last. If you prefer to skip around, though, go right ahead. Read the dialogues first or save them for later. Or use the index to look up particular words of interest.

Finally, I would like to express my appreciation to Kodansha International editors Michael Brase and Shigeyoshi Suzuki, who encouraged me to write this unwritable book, and to the translator, Tom Gally, who was the book's first reader and, at times, its first critic.

Thanks must also go to the people from many countries of the world who were my students at the Bunka Institute of Language and elsewhere, to the Japanese people I have met over the years who have used the language in all its wonderful variety, and most of all to you, the unseen reader, as we embark together on a voyage into the world of sound and action words in Japanese.

*Don't let these two terms scare you. In Japanese, they're a bit easier to understand. Onomatopoeia is 擬音語 *gion-go*, literally, "a word that imitates a sound," and mimesis is 擬態語 *gitai-go*, literally, "a word that imitates an action or state." English has many examples of both: bang, crunch, hiss, thunk, and crackle are all onomatopoeia, while flip, gooey, slither, sparkle, and slip are mimesis.

A New Lease on Life

Tetsu Takahashi of the Marketing Department at Heiwa Securities and his boss, Section Chief Hideo Satō, drop by a bar after work. The beer has just arrived.

12

A New Lease on Life

高橋 「きょうは参りました*ね、課長。もう**へとへと**ですよ。」

佐藤 「**がんがん**飲もう。俺がおごるよ。」

高橋 「はあ。ありがとうございます。まあどうぞ。」
 　　（課長のグラスにビールを注ぐ†。ビールがあふれそう
 　　になって）

佐藤 「おうっとっと。……**きりきり**することばっかりで、喉
 　　も**からから**だな。」

高橋 「全くですね。一日中**どたばた**して、**ぺこぺこ**頭をさげ
 　　まわって。」
 　　（佐藤さんにビールを注ぎながら）

佐藤 「ま、こういうときには、**じたばた**したって駄目なもん
 　　だよ。」

高橋 「はあ、どうも。（注がれたビールを一口飲んで）……
 　　うまい。冷えてる。やっぱり**すかっと**しますね、ビール
 　　は。」

佐藤 「**ちびちび**飲んでないで、**ぐうっと**いこうよ、**ぐうっ
 　　と**。」
 　　（さらに高橋さんにビールを注ぐと、高橋さんは勢いよ
 　　く飲み干して♦）

高橋 「課長こそ**どんどん**いきましょう。」
 　　（佐藤課長、このところ目立ってきたおなかをさすりな
 　　がら）

佐藤 「**どんどん**はいいけど、水を飲んでも太る体質♣でね。
 　　まあいいか、きょうのところは。」
 　　（課長にビールを注ぎ終えたところに、注文したおつま
 　　みがくる）

店員 「へい、お待ちどう、焼き鳥5人前。」

---

　* *Mairu*: to be beaten, defeated, frustrated.
　† *Tsugu*: to pour.
　♦ *Nomihosu*: to drink to the last drop.
　♣ *Taishitsu*: constitution, physical type.

Takahashi: *Kyō wa mairimashita ne, kachō. Mō hetoheto desu yo.*

Satō: *Gangan nomō. Ore ga ogoru yo.*

Takahashi: *Hā. Arigatō gozaimasu. Mā dōzo.*

          (Kachō no gurasu ni bīru o tsugu. Bīru ga afuresō ni natte.)

Satō: *Ōttotto.... Kirikiri suru koto bakkari de, nodo mo kara-kara da na.*

Takahashi: *Mattaku desu ne. Ichinichi-jū dotabata shite, pekopeko atama o sagemawatte.*

          (Satō-san ni bīru o tsuginagara)

Satō: *Ma, kō iu toki ni wa, jitabata shita tte dame na mon da yo.*

Takahashi: *Hā, dōmo. (Tsugareta bīru o hitokuchi nonde) …Umai. Hiete 'ru. Yappari sukatto shimasu ne, bīru wa.*

Satō: *Chibichibi nonde 'nai de, gūtto ikō yo, gūtto.*

          (Sara ni Takahashi-san ni bīru o tsugu to, Takahashi-san wa ikiyoi yoku nomihoshite)

Takahashi: *Kachō koso dondon ikimashō.*

          (Satō-kachō, konogoro medatte kita onaka o sasurinagara)

Satō: *Dondon wa ii kedo, mizu o nonde mo futoru taishitsu de ne. Mā ii ka, kyō no tokoro wa.*

          (Kachō ni bīru o tsugioeta tokoro ni, chūmon shita otsumami ga kuru.)

Ten'in: *Hei, omachi-dō, yakitori gonin-mae.*

★

Takahashi: Today was a real killer, wasn't it, boss. I'm dead tired.

Satō: What do you say we knock back a few. It's on me.

Takahashi: Hey, thanks a lot. Here you go. (He pours beer into Satō's glass, almost to overflowing.)

Satō: Whoa, watch it there.… It's been one thing after another, and my throat's gone bone-dry.

Takahashi: The same here. I've been on the go all day long, out talking up clients.

Satō   (pouring for Takahashi): Well, this is not the time or
          place to be twiddling our thumbs.

Takahashi: Okay, thanks. (He takes a drink.) Aah, that's nice and
          cold. Beer sure hits the spot.

Satō: Don't just sip at it! Down the hatch! (Satō fills Taka-
          hashi's glass again, and he empties it enthusiastically.)

Takahashi: Come on. You, too, boss. Drink up.

Satō   (rubbing his belly, which has become more noticeable
          recently): I like my drink as much as the next man, but I
          put on weight just from drinking water. Oh, well, only
          for tonight.

          (Just as Takahashi finishes pouring some more beer for
          Satō, the food they ordered arrives.)

Waiter: Here you are. Yakitori for five.

➥ Employees of Japanese companies and other organizations rarely
address each other by their given names. They generally use surnames
followed by a title (社長、部長、課長、係長, etc.). When there's no possi-
bility of confusion, the family name can be dropped.

   When drinking socially, people usually pour drinks for one another. In
this dialogue, Takahashi pours the first round because he is the lower
ranking of the two. For later rounds, either one might pour for the other.

へとへと (hetoheto) N / B

To be completely tired, worn out, exhausted.

❑ 2時間もラッシュの電車に乗って通勤すると、会社に着く頃にはも
   うへとへとですよ。

*Ni-jikan mo rasshu no densha ni notte tsūkin suru to, kaisha ni tsuku
koro wa mō hetoheto desu yo.*

After a two-hour train commute during the morning rush, I'm dead on
my feet by the time I reach the office.

❑ やっぱり運動不足なんだね。子供の運動会でちょっと走ったらへと
   へとになったよ。

*Yappari undō-busoku nan da ne. Kodomo no undō-kai de chotto hashit-
tara hetoheto ni natta yo.*

Sure enough, I'm not getting the exercise I should. Just running a little at
my kid's sports festival completely wiped me out.

がんがん (gangan) N / B

This word describes an extremely strong or violent action.

❑ 席を移ってもいいかしら、冷房ががんがんきいていて落ち着かない
  んですもの。

*Seki o utsutte mo ii kashira, reibō ga gangan kiite ite ochitsukanai n'
desu mono.*

Would you mind if I changed seats? With the air conditioning going full
  blast, I'm beginning to feel absolutely uncomfortable.

❑ 浮気がばれて女房にがんがんしぼられまして*ね、当分頭が上がり
  ません。

*Uwaki ga barete nyōbō ni gangan shiboraremashite ne, tōbun atama ga
agarimasen.*

When my wife found out I was running around with someone else, she
  lowered the boom. Now she's got me under her thumb.

  * *Shiboru*: to wring, tighten the screws on.

きりきり (kirikiri) N / B

The original meaning of this word is the creaking or scraping sound
caused by something being rotated, wrapped, or tightened. It can also
describe the motion itself. By extension, *kirikiri* sometimes means
"very busy," including the notion of stress or tension caused by haste
or impatience (N/B). Another meaning is a sharp, continuous pain, as
though a pointed object were being forced into one's body (B).

❑ 忙しいからときりきりしたところで、結果はそう変わらないんです
  けどね。

*Isogashii kara to kirikiri shita tokoro de, kekka wa sō kawaranai n' desu
kedo ne.*

Just because you're busy and work yourself into a frenzy (work your fingers to the bone), the results aren't all that different, it seems.

❑ 部長の雷が落ちる*たびに、胃がきりきり痛むんです。

Buchō no kaminari ga ochiru tabi ni, i ga kirikiri itamu n' desu.

Every time the division manager goes on one of his rampages, my stomach gets all tied up in knots (starts acting up).

  * *Kaminari ga ochiru*: to thunder, scold.

からから (karakara) N / B

Completely dry, containing no moisture.

❑ 独身はわびしいですよ。出張から帰ってくると、観葉植物*までか
  らからに枯れているんだから。

Dokushin wa wabishii desu yo. Shutchō kara kaette kuru to, kan'yō-shokubutsu made karakara ni karete iru n' da kara.

Being single is really pathetic. Whenever I come home from a business trip, even my plants are all withered.

> * *Kan'yō-shokubutsu*: potted (ornamental) plants.

❑ 東京の冬は風邪がはやっても無理ないですね。空気がからからで喉をいためるんですよ。

Tōkyō no fuyu wa kaze ga hayatte mo muri nai desu ne. Kūki ga karakara de nodo o itameru n' desu yo.

It's no wonder so many people in Tokyo get colds during the winter. The air's bone-dry and raises havoc with your throat.

どたばた (dotabata) B

This word describes the sound or action of flying, jumping, or running around. By extension, it also means to rush wildly from place to place without being able to settle down. The word sometimes suggests a criticism of the person performing such an action or of the action itself. When used by the speaker about himself or his associates, it includes a sense of humility and embarrassment.

❑ うちでは子供がどたばたしているもので、落ち着いて本も読めないんですよ。

Uchi de wa kodomo ga dotabata shite iru mono de, ochitsuite hon mo yomenai n' desu yo.

With the children rampaging around the house, I can't get enough peace and quiet to even read a book.

❑ きょうは社内の引っ越しで一日中どたばたしてしまいましてね、仕事にならなかったんですよ。

Kyō wa shanai no hikkoshi de ichinichi-jū dotabata shite shimaimashite ne, shigoto ni naranakatta n' desu yo.

Today was moving day at the office, so everyone was running around like chickens with their heads cut off. Nobody got a bit of work done.

ぺこぺこ (pekopeko) B

To bow one's head repeatedly in a fawning or groveling manner.

❑ 営業をやっている悲しさで、つい誰にでもぺこぺこしてしまうんですよ。

Eigyō o yatte iru kanashisa de, tsui dare ni de mo pekopeko shite shimau n' desu yo.

The sad part of being in sales is that you end up bowing and scraping to anything that moves.

❏ あなた、ぺこぺこ謝ってばかりいないで、何とか言ったらどうなの。

Anata, pekopeko ayamatte bakari inai de, nan to ka ittara dō na no.

Listen, honey. Don't just stand there apologizing like a fool. Explain
yourself.

➡ As a sign of respect, bowing (お辞儀 *ojigi*) is deeply ingrained in Japanese life. People bow to greet others, to say good-bye, to show respect, to
make a request, and to apologize. With so many uses, it's natural that
there should be many types of bows. The three main categories, depend-
ing on the angle of the bow, are 会釈 *eshaku*, a slight bow, a nod of the
head; 敬礼 *keirei*, a full bow, a respectful bow; and 最敬礼 *saikeirei*, a
very low bow, a worshipful bow. The deeper the bow, the greater the
respect.

When standing up, you can do an *eshaku* just by tipping your head
forward slightly. This casual bow is appropriate, for example, when
greeting an acquaintance on the street. For the more formal *keirei*, stand
with heels together and toes slightly spread, look at the ground about a
yard in front of you, and bow from the waist. Men usually keep their
arms straight down at their sides, while women let their arms swing forward naturally as they bow. The deepest, most respectful bow, *saikeirei*,
is performed from a motionless standing position, with the body bent
sharply at the waist and the arms held straight down toward the knees.
This bow was originally reserved for gods or emperors, though now you
may see it employed on other formal occasions as well.

If seated on the floor, take the 正座 *seiza* position (legs folded under,
knees together, bottom resting on your feet, back straight, and, ideally,
one of your big toes resting on the other), place your hands on the floor
in front of you, and bow from the waist with your face pointed toward
your hands. For the *eshaku*, bend your body forward about 15°; for the
keirei, about 45°; and for the *saikeirei*, until your nose is nearly touching
your hands.

The most common mistake non-Japanese make when bowing is to
bend from the neck. While you may amuse your friends with your imita-
tion of a goose, you're better off, for all but the most casual *eshaku*, if
you bend from the waist. Another mistake, made by Japanese as well, is
to bow more than necessary. Repeated bowing is appropriate when apologizing or making requests, but overly enthusiastic bowing—and this is
the nuance of *pekopeko*—gives the impression of being unnecessarily
servile.

じたばた (jitabata) B
To flail around one's arms and legs. By extension, to panic or become flustered when trying to confront some imminent problem.

❑ うちの子、歯医者さんが嫌いでね、手足をじたばたさせて抵抗する から困るわ。

Uchi no ko, haisha-san ga kirai de ne, te-ashi o jitabata sasete teikō suru kara komaru wa.

Our kid really hates the dentist. He wriggles like the dickens and simply refuses to cooperate.

❑ 何をやってもうまくいかないときには、じたばたしない方が賢明で すよ。

Nani o yatte mo umaku ikanai toki ni wa, jitabata shinai hō ga kenmei desu yo.

When things don't work out no matter what, you're better off just staying cool and collected.

すかっと (sukatto) G

Clear, refreshing. Free from bad feelings.

❑ 山に登ってすかっとした青空を見ていると、気持ちまですかっとし ますよ。

Yama ni nobotte sukatto shita aozora o mite iru to, kimochi made sukatto shimasu yo.

When you climb to the top of a mountain and look up into a clear, blue sky, you can't help feeling like a new man (like a million bucks).

❑ 友達と長電話して愚痴*を聞いてもらったら、すかっとしたわ。

Tomodachi to naga-denwa shite guchi o kiite morattara, sukatto shita wa.

I had a long talk with a friend over the phone and got a lot out of my system. Now I really feel great (on top of the world).

  * *Guchi*: complaints, grievances.

❑ ゆうべ飲み過ぎましてね、けさからどうもすかっとしないんです。

Yūbe nomisugimashite ne, kesa kara dōmo sukatto shinai n' desu.

I drank too much last night and just don't feel myself today.

ちびちび (chibichibi) N / B

To do something slowly and steadily, not all at once. Sometimes used to suggest stinginess.

❑ 日本酒は寿司屋で寿司を握ってもらいながらちびちび飲むのが最高 ですよ。

Nihon-shu wa sushi-ya de sushi o nigitte morainagara chibichibi nomu no ga saikō desu yo.

There's nothing like sipping away at your sake in a sushi shop while they're making the sushi for you.

❏ 僕はちびちび倹約するというのが苦手で、いつも女房にしかられているんです。

Boku wa chibichibi ken'yaku suru to iu no ga nigate de, itsumo nyōbō ni shikararete iru n' desu.

My wife always bawls me out because I'm no good at pinching pennies.

ぐうっと／ぐっと (gūtto/gutto) G / N

The basic meaning of these two words is to concentrate all one's energy to perform an action (N). They can also be used to express a big change or difference from a preceding condition or a strong emotion (N) or a feeling that seems to take one's breath way (G/N). *Gūtto* and *gutto* are synonymous, but the former expresses a stronger or more prolonged action, change, or emotion.

❏ 彼の言動*には頭にくるでしょうが、そこはぐっとこらえてください。

Kare no gendō ni wa atama ni kuru deshō ga, soko wa gutto koraete kudasai.

His behavior probably pisses you off, but try not to let it get you down.

   * *Gendō*: speech and action.

❏ 美恵子ちゃん、大学に入ったら、ぐうっと大人びちゃって*見違えたよ。

Mieko-chan, daigaku ni haittara, gūtto otonabichatte michigaeta yo.

Since Mieko started college, she's suddenly starting acting so adult she seems like a different person (you wouldn't recognize her).

   * *Otonabiru*: to look and act grown-up.

❏ 目に涙をためて彼女に謝られたときには、ぐうっときちゃったね。

Me ni namida o tamete kanojo ni ayamarareta toki ni wa, gūtto kichatta ne.

She had tears in her eyes when she said she was sorry. It really got to me.

どんどん (dondon) N

This word describes an action that proceeds continuously and vigorously from one step to the next, without delay or hesitation.

❏ サラリーマンはつまりません*よ、働けば働いただけどんどん儲かるというのならいいんですがね。

Sararīman wa tsumarimasen yo, hatarakeba hataraita dake dondon mōkaru to iu no nara ii n' desu ga ne.

It's a drag being a salaryman. I only wish the money would come in as fast as I'm scrambling to make it.

* *Tsumarimasen (tsumaranai):* boring, tedious.

❏ お父さんと買い物にいくのはいやだわ。だってひとりでどんどん勝手に行っちゃうんだもの。

Otōsan to kaimono ni iku no wa iya da wa. Datte hitori de dondon katte ni itchau n' da mono.

I hate going shopping with my dad. He just barges on ahead all by himself.

A Business Lunch

Ken'ichi Yamamoto of the Tokyo trading house Meiji Shōkai is discussing business over lunch with Tadashi Horiuchi of the trading house Shōwa Shōji, which is headquartered in Osaka.

A Business Lunch

堀内　「もうかりまっか。」

山本　「まあまあですね。でも下半期は**がくんと**落ち込むんじゃないですか。営業は**ぴりぴり**してますよ。おたく*はどうですか。」

堀内　「やあ、**ぼちぼち**でんな。うちとこも**うかうか**してられまへんわ。」

山本　「どこでも同じですね。ところで例の†件ですが、予算が**きちきち**で……。この間の額で何とかなりませんか。お支払いは**きちんと**しますから。」

堀内　「そうですかあ。いやあ、難儀ですなあ。うちも**ぎりぎり**でんねん。」

山本　「そこのところを何とかのんで*いただけないでしょうか。この通りです。✿」（と山本さんが頭を下げる）

堀内　「つろおますなあ、山本さんにそない言われたら。そやけど**すんなり**はいどうぞ、言うわけにもいきまへんやろ。こっちのつらい立場もわかってほしおますなあ。」

山本　「それはごもっとも✚です。しかし、堀内さん、困りましたねえ……。」

堀内　「ほな、よろしおます。これ以上**ずるずる**延ばすわけにもいきまへんやろし、勉強さしてもろて、端数を**すっぱり**切り捨てるいうことでどないでっしょ。」

山本　「そこまでおっしゃるのなら、**ずばり**その線で✚手を打ちましょう。よろしくお願いします。そうと決まったら、どうです。ひとつビールでも。」

堀内　「おおきに。あんじょうたのんまっさ。」

---

* *Otaku*: somewhat respectful term for someone of approximately the same status but with whom one is not on the most intimate terms: "you, your family, your place of business."

† *Rei no*: (the matter) in question.

✧ *Nomu*: agree to, accept.

✿ *Kono tōri desu*: "(I am) in this manner"; said when bowing and asking a favor.

✚ *(Go)mottomo*: natural, understandable, justifiable.

✚ *Sono sen de*: along those lines.

Horiuchi: *Mōkarimakka.*

Yamamoto: *Māmā desu ne. Demo shimohan-ki wa gakunto ochiko-mu n' ja nai desu ka. Eigyō wa piripiri shite 'masu yo. Otaku wa dō desu ka.*

Horiuchi: *Yā, bochibochi den na. Uchi toko mo ukauka shite 'raremahen wa.*

Yamamoto: *Doko de mo onaji desu ne. Tokoro de rei no ken desu ga, yosan ga kichikichi de.... Kono aida no gaku de nan to ka narimasen ka. Oshiharai wa kichinto shimasu kara.*

Horiuchi: *Sō desu kā. Iyā, nangi desu nā. Uchi mo girigiri den nen.*

Yamamoto: *Soko no tokoro o nan to ka nonde itadakenai deshō ka. Kono tōri desu. (to Yamamoto-san ga atama o sageru)*

Horiuchi: *Tsurō 'masu nā, Yamamoto-san ni sonai iwaretara. Soyakedo sunnari hai dōzo, iu wake ni mo ikimahen yaro. Kotchi no tsurai tachiba mo wakatte hoshi omasu nā.*

Yamamoto: *Sore wa gomottomo desu. Shikashi, Horiuchi-san, Ko-marimashita nē.*

Horiuchi: *Hona, yoroshi omasu. Kore ijō zuruzuru nobasu wake ni mo ikimahen yaro shi, benkyō sashite morote, hasū o suppari kirisuteru iu koto de donai dessharo.*

Yamamoto: *Soko made ossharu no nara, zubari sono sen de te o uchimashō. Yoroshiku onegai shimasu. Sō to kimattara, dō desu. Hitotsu bīru de mo.*

Horiuchi: *Ōki ni. Anjō tanonmassa.*

☆

Horiuchi: How's business?

Yamamoto: Pretty good. But it looks as though we're in for a tumble in the second half (of the fiscal year). Our sales people are starting to get jittery. How are things at your place?

Horiuchi: We're managing somehow, but we'll have to keep on our toes, too.

Yamamoto: It's the same all over. Now, about that deal, our budget is tight as a drum.... And the price you mentioned, do you think you could do something about that? We'll pay promptly, right on the dot.

Horiuchi: Well, well, well. That places me in a difficult position. Our profit margin would be cut to the bone.

Yamamoto: Can't you find some way to work around that? As a favor to me. (Yamamoto bows his head.)

Horiuchi: That really puts me on the spot, expressing it like that. You know, I can't say, "Sure, fine with me," just like that. You need to understand how tough our situation is here.

Yamamoto: I get your point, but now that really pushes me against the wall.

Horiuchi: All right, then. We can't let this drag on forever. I'll offer you a discount. Suppose we just round off the price?

Yamamoto: If you're willing to go with that, it's settled. Now that that's out of the way (concluded), how about a beer?

Horiuchi: Thanks. It's a deal.

➡ If Horiuchi's conversation seems strange to you, that's because he's speaking the Osaka dialect of Japanese. His first question, もうかりまっか (もうかりますか in standard Japanese), is a customary greeting in Osaka, meaning "Have you been making a lot of money?" To a Tokyo-ite, such a direct reference to money-making would seem a bit gauche; businesspeople in the capital instead might say 景気はどうですか, which literally means, "How is the economic situation?"

Horiuchi's second statement could be rendered into standard Japanese as いやあ、まあまあですね。私どももうかうかしていられませんよ. The Osaka でんな would be ですな in Tokyo, and the standard *s* in the negative suffix becomes *h*: ～まへん = ～ません. Horiuchi's third line corresponds to そうですか。いやあ、困りましたね。うちもぎりぎりなんですよ in Tokyo dialect.

His fourth line can be rendered as つらいですね。山本さんにそう頼まれると。しかしねえ、すんなりはいどうぞ、と言うわけにもいかないでしょう。こちらのつらい立場もわかっていただきたいですね. Here, つろおます means つらいです and ほしおます means ほしいです. Similarly, そない corresponds to そんな（ふう）に and そやけど to そうだけど.

Horiuchi's fifth line becomes the following in Tokyo: それなら結構です。これ以上ずるずる延ばすわけにはいかないでしょうし、値引きさせていただいて、端数をすっぱり切り捨てるということでどうでしょう. Notice that やろ corresponds to だろう or でしょう. The phrase 勉強さし

てもろて means 勉強させてもらって, but be careful: 勉強する does not mean "to study" here; the phrase has an additional slang meaning, in both Osaka dialect and standard Japanese, of "to lower the price, to make a discount."

Horiuchi's closing speech, おおきに。あんじょうたのんまっさ, can be rendered as ありがとうございます。よろしくお願いします. The word あんじょう comes from 味良く, meaning "good, well," which, of course, is the origin of よろしく

The version of Japanese taught to foreigners is nearly always 標準語 *hyōjun-go* "standard Japanese," which is very close to the dialect spoken in the Tokyo area. But as the above conversation shows, people in Osaka speak very differently. In fact, from Hokkaido in the north to Okinawa in the south, Japanese has dozens of distinct dialects, each with its own accent, intonation, and vocabulary. While all Japanese people understand *hyōjun-go*—after all, it is the language of television, radio, and written Japanese—the language they speak in their daily lives varies greatly from region to region. In some areas, such as Tohoku and Kagoshima, the local dialect may be nearly incomprehensible to people from other parts of Japan.

For centuries, the Kansai area, which encompasses Osaka and Kyoto, was the economic and political center of Japan. The distinctive culture and way of life that developed in the region are reflected today in its unique style of speaking. Though it's difficult to convey in writing the full flavor of 大阪弁 *Ōsaka-ben*, here are a few examples:

OSAKA	TOKYO	ENGLISH
ōkini	*arigatō*	thank you
sainara	*sayōnara*	good-bye
gyōsan	*takusan*	many, much
homma	*hontō*	really
omoroi	*omoshiroi*	interesting, fun
donai	*dō, dono yō ni*	how?
wa (both men's and women's speech)	*wa* (women's speech) *yo* (men's speech)	declarative particle

➡ In Japanese, indirect expressions and roundabout ways of talking are often considered more grown-up and sophisticated. This linguistic style appears even in business negotiations, which often proceed without any mention of specific prices or conditions. While this works fine when both parties understand each other, someone who is not used to this type of discussion—particularly a foreigner—may feel confused or even deceived by the lack of concrete information.

The above dialogue between Horiuchi and Yamamoto is a good example. Their conversation is rich with expressions that would be opaque to any outsider: 「予算がきちきち」「この間の額」「お支払いはきちんと」「うちもぎりぎり」「端数をすっぱり切り捨てる」「ずばりその線で」。 A phrase used in Yamamoto's second statement—例の件—makes it clear that they have discussed this deal before and that Yamamoto proposed a specific price. Horiuchi is reluctant to accept that price—難儀ですなあ—so Yamamoto urges him to accept the stated conditions. When Yamamoto bows his head, he "stoops to conquer": rather than putting pressure on the other man, he wants Horiuchi to feel that he would be doing Yamamoto a favor.

Horiuchi shows that he understands Yamamoto's position—つろおますなあ、山本さんにそない言われたら—but by saying そやけどすんなりはいどうぞ、言うわけにもいきまへんやろ。こっちのつらい立場もわかってほしおますなあ、he makes it clear that he won't be able to accept Yamamoto's proposal. Yamamoto shows that he also understands Horiuchi's point of view, but he can't accept it, either—that's the meaning of 困りましたねえ…。It's at this point that Horiuchi proposes the compromise that closes the deal—端数をすっぱり切り捨てるいうことでどないでっしゃろ—but even then the final amount is not mentioned, just that they will "round off the price."

がくんと (gakunto) N / B

To fold, bend, collapse, crack, split, or budge, often because of a sudden shock. Also used to describe a sudden loss of energy or spirit.

❏ 夏休みに遊びすぎたのがたたって*、がくんと成績が落ちちゃったよ。

Natsu-yasumi ni asobisugita no ga tatatte, gakunto seiseki ga ochichatta yo.

I got what I deserved for fooling around too much during summer vacation: my grades went into a tailspin.

　　* *Tataru*: to be cursed, ruined, suffer (because of something).

❏ 電車ががくんと急停車したものだから、みんな将棋倒しになっちゃったのよ。

Densha ga gakunto kyū-teisha shita mono da kara, minna shōgi-daoshi ni natchatta no yo.

When the train came lurching to a stop, everyone was knocked flat like a bunch of dominoes (shōgi pieces).

ぴりぴり (piripiri) N / B

(1) A sharp feeling of pain, spiciness, electric shock, etc. on the skin, tongue, nose, etc. (2) To become nervous, high-strung, or oversensitive because of fear, unease, tension, etc.

❑ このキムチ、おいしいけど辛いわね。舌にぴりぴりくるわ。

Kono kimuchi, oishii kedo karai wa ne. Shita ni piripiri kuru wa.

This kimchi tastes good, but it sure is spicy. My tongue's on fire.

❑ 子供のいたずらくらいで、そんなにぴりぴり神経をとがらせる*なよ。

Kodomo no itazura kurai de, sonna ni piripiri shinkei o togaraseru na yo.

Don't get so uptight over some kid's prank.

　　* *Togaraseru*: to sharpen, put on edge.

ぼちぼち／ぽちぽち (bochibochi/pochipochi) N

(1) Gradually; slowly but steadily. (2) Used to describe something that is about to happen. Imminently. Right away. (3) The condition of many dots or other small objects scattered around. While *bochibochi* and *pochipochi* are nearly identical, *bochibochi* conveys somewhat more emphasis.

❑ 土日を利用してぼちぼち書いてるから、いっこうに*年賀状、書き終わらないよ。

Donichi o riyō shite bochibochi kaite 'ru kara, ikkō ni nenga-jō, kaki-owaranai yo.

Since I can only plug away at my New Year's cards on the weekends, it seems I'll never finish.

　　* *Ikkō ni*: (not) at all, (not) a bit.

❑ 雨も上がったし、ぼちぼち出かけようか。

Ame mo agatta shi, bochibochi dekakeyō ka.

The rain's stopped, so let's get going.

❑ このテーブルクロス、ぽちぽちしみがついているから、取り替えましょう。

Kono tēburukurosu, pochipochi shimi ga tsuite iru kara, torikaemashō.

This tablecloth is all stained with spots. Let's change it.

➡ *Nenga-jō* (年賀状) are postcards that people send at the end of each year to their friends, colleagues, and business contacts. While the size of the postcards is standardized, their design and content are not. Many people make their own drawings or prints, often incorporating a picture of the animal that symbolizes the coming year, and the text may vary from a brief formal greeting to a lengthy handwritten message. Parents of small children often attach photos of their offspring.

Most people put their messages on blank cards that are sold each year at the post office. Lottery numbers appear along the bottom of each card, so the people who receive the cards get a chance at winning prizes ranging from a small sheet of stamps to a television or video deck.

Someone with a large circle of acquaintances may send and receive several hundred cards each year. The month of December is thus a busy time as everyone hurries to prepare their New Year's cards. The payback comes on New Year's Day, when the post office makes a special delivery of only New Year's cards, which can be read and enjoyed at leisure through the holidays.

One warning: As a sign of mourning, people who have lost a close relative during the preceding year do not send New Year's cards. Nor does one send a card when this fact is known.

うかうか (ukauka) B

To be careless, absentminded.

❑ すごい人ごみだね。うかうかしていると迷子になりそうだよ。

Sugoi hitogomi da ne. Ukauka shite iru to maigo ni narisō da yo.

What a crowd! You could end up getting lost if you don't watch out.

❑ 来年はもう就職だし、うかうかしてはいられないわ。

Rainen wa mō shūshoku da shi, ukauka shite wa irarenai wa.

I have to look for a job next year, so I can't afford to be fooling around (let things slide) now.

きちきち (kichikichi) N / B

To be full, to have no leeway, to be at the limit.

❑ このおまんじゅう、箱にきちきちに詰まってるわね。

Kono omanjū, hako ni kichikichi ni tsumatte 'ru wa ne.

These *manjū* buns sure are jam-packed into the box.

❑ せっかく海外に行っても、出張じゃスケジュールがきちきちだから ちっとも楽しめないよ。

Sekkaku kaigai ni itte mo, shutchō ja sukejūru ga kichikichi da kara chitto mo tanoshimenai yo.

Now that I've finally gotten a chance to go overseas, it's only a business trip. My schedule is so tight that I won't have any time for fun.

➡ A *manjū* (まんじゅう) is made of a sweet bean paste called あん *an* (or, more informally, あんこ *anko*) that is wrapped in dough and then steamed or roasted. Imported from China by a Buddhist priest in the thirteenth century, the recipe spread throughout Japan in later years and became one of the most popular types of pastry.

きちんと (kichinto) G

Carefully, neatly, accurately, fully, properly.

❏ 布団は、朝起きたらきちんとたたんで押し入れに入れておいてください。

Futon wa, asa okitara kichinto tatande oshi-ire ni irete oite kudasai.

As soon as you wake up in the morning, fold your futon neatly and put it in the closet.

❏ 伊藤さんはきちんとしているから、待ち合わせに遅れるはずないよ。

Itō-san wa kichinto shite iru kara, machiawase ni okureru hazu nai yo.

Mr. Itō is a very reliable person. I can't see him being late to the meeting.

➥ There are two types of futon in Japan, the *shikibuton* (敷き布団), a relatively thick mattress usually filled with cotton batting, and the *kakebuton* (掛け布団), a lighter quilt filled with cotton, down, wool, polyester, etc. The sleeper lies on the *shikibuton*, which is placed directly on the tatami, floor, or carpet, and the *kakebuton* is used as a blanket.

While beds are becoming more common in Japan, futons retain their popularity because of their convenience. In the morning, they can be folded up and put in the closet, thus freeing the sleeping room for other uses during the day. The closets, called *oshi-ire* (押し入れ), are designed for this purpose, for they typically have a large, flat shelf at about waist height where the futons can be stacked.

ぎりぎり (girigiri) N

With almost no time, space, or leeway to spare. Similar in meaning to *kichikichi*, but *girigiri* emphasizes even more strongly that the ultimate limit has been reached.

❏ ドアが閉まるぎりぎりでかけこみ乗車*して、けがでもしたらどうするの。

Doa ga shimaru girigiri de kakekomi-jōsha shite, kega de mo shitara dō suru no.

Are you trying to hurt yourself or something, rushing into the train at the very last second like that?

　* *Kakekomi-jōsha*: rushing onto a train to beat the closing doors.

❏ 給料をもらっても、家のローンを支払っているんで生活費ぎりぎりしか残らないんですよ。

Kyūryō o moratte mo, ie no rōn o shiharatte iru n' de seikatsu-hi girigiri shika nokoranai n' desu yo.

After paying our home loan, I have barely enough left over from my salary to pay our living expenses.

すんなり (sunnari) G

(1) Slender, smooth, graceful. While *surari* suggests something that is long and straight, *sunnari* emphasizes that the object is also flexible. (2) *Sunnari* is also used to describe something that proceeds smoothly even though some resistance is expected.

❑ 中村さんの指って、すんなりとしていてきれいね。指輪がひきたつわ。

Nakamura-san no yubi tte, sunnari to shite ite kirei ne. Yubiwa ga hiki-tatsu wa.

Your fingers are so nice and slender, Miss Nakamura; they set off your ring very nicely.

❑ もっと高速*が渋滞するかと思ったけど、案外†すんなり通れたね。

Motto kōsoku ga jūtai suru ka to omotta kedo, angai sunnari tōreta ne.

I thought the expressway would be more crowded, but we breezed through without much trouble.

* *Kōsoku*: abbreviation of 高速道路 *kōsoku-dōro*.
† *Angai*: surprisingly, unexpectedly.

❑ こっちの言い分をすんなりわかってくれるような人なら、誰も苦労なんかしませんよ。

Kotchi no iibun o sunnari wakatte kureru yō na hito nara, dare mo kurō nanka shimasen yo.

If he could just get what I'm saying through his thick skull, then he wouldn't be such a pain in the neck.

ずるずる (zuruzuru) B

(1) The sound or feeling of a long or heavy object being pulled, dragged, or slid. (2) The sound or appearance of slurping, snuffling, sniffing—that is, inhaling a wet object or substance (soba noodles, mucus, etc.). (3) To slip, fall, collapse; to be unable to maintain a fixed position. (4) To dawdle, to let a bad situation drag on, to be unable to reach a satisfactory conclusion. Except when used to describe noodle eating, *zuruzuru* generally has a negative connotation of slackness or laziness.

❑ 靴ひもをずるずる引きずって歩いていると、危ないですよ。

Kutsuhimo o zuruzuru hikizutte aruite iru to, abunai desu yo.

It's dangerous to walk around dragging your shoelaces like that.

❏ 鼻をずるずるすすっていないで、ちゃんとかみなさい。

Hana o zuruzuru susutte inai de, chanto kaminasai.

Stop all that sniffling and blow your nose.

❏ この靴下、ずるずるずり落ちて困るんだ。

Kono kutsushita, zuruzuru zuriochite komaru n' da.

I hate these socks because they keep sliding down.

❏ すぐ失礼するつもりだったんですけど、ついずるずる長居*をして
しまってすみません。

*Sugu shitsurei suru tsumori datta n' desu kedo, tsui zuruzuru nagai o
shite shimatte sumimasen.*

I'm afraid I've worn out my welcome. I hadn't intended to stay so long.

* *Nagai*: an unconscionably long visit.

すっぱり (suppari) G / N

(1) To cut, break, or separate sharply and neatly. (2) To arrange a
matter decisively and permanently so that nothing undone remains.
Used particularly when quitting or giving something up.

❏ 植木屋さんが枝をすっぱり払ってくれたのはいいけど、何だか寒々
としちゃったわね。

*Uekiya-san ga eda o suppari haratte kureta no wa ii kedo, nan da ka
samuzamu to shichatta wa ne.*

True, the gardener cut back the branches very nicely, but now the tree
looks so forlorn.

❏ 胃かいようを患ってから、酒はすっぱりやめたんだ。

I-kaiyō o wazuratte kara, sake wa suppari yameta n' da.

I went cold turkey on the alcohol after I got an ulcer.

ずばり (zubari) G / N

(1) To cut, slice, or strike something with a single sharp blow. While
suppari suggests that the object is completely severed, *zubari* can be
used even when the cut is not complete. Often *zubari* emphasizes the
accuracy of the action. (2) To go to the core of a subject, to be right
on target. Often used to describe a plain, direct manner of speaking
that gets straight to the point or an insight that reveals a hidden truth.

❏ 剣道はやはりこわいですよ。一瞬のすきを、ずばり打ちこまれます
からね。

Kendō wa yahari kowai desu yo. Isshun no suki o, zubari uchikomarema-
su kara ne.

I think kendō is really scary. Give your opponent the slightest opening
and he'll score a hit.

❏ あそこの占いはずばりと当たるって評判なのよ。

Asoko no uranai wa zubari to ataru tte hyōban na no yo.

They say that fortune-teller is always right on the money.

A Man's Place

Mari Wakabayashi and Harumi Yamato are nodding acquaintances at their fitness club. They have a chat as they work out on exercise machines.

A Man's Place

大和　「**こんがり**焼けていらっしゃいますね。海ですか。」

若林　「ええ、プーケットに行ってきたんです。焼き過ぎてま　　だ**ひりひり***しちゃって。」

大和　「いいですね。ご主人とご一緒に？」

若林　「ええまあ。」

大和　「うらやましいわ。うちなんか、夏休みも結局家で**ごろ　　ごろ**しているだけ。近頃**ぶくぶく**太ってきちゃって。　　それにしても、ご精が出ます†ね。」

若林　「トライアスロンをやっているものですから。」

大和　「えっ、あの鉄人レースの？　すごいわあ。」

若林　「すごくないんですよ。ジョギングから始めて、**じりじ　　り**と距離を伸ばしていって……。**こつこつ**練習すれば、　　誰にでもできますよ。」

大和　「じゃあ、プーケットでも、トレーニングを？」

若林　「もちろん。」

大和　「道理で❖**すらり**としていらっしゃると思ったわ。ご主　　人もやっぱり？」

若林　「いいえ、うちのは**ずんぐりむっくり**の純日本型。学生　　時代は相撲部ですもの。」

大和　「まあ、**がっしり**していていいじゃありませんの。トレ　　ーニングにも付き合ってくださるんでしょう？」

若林　「まさか。機内では**ぐっすり**、ホテルでは**ぐったり**、海　　辺では**ごろごろ**していただけですわ。」

---

* *Hirihiri*: see "Feeling Out of Sorts?"

† *Sei ga deru*: energy comes forth; to be energetic.

❖ *Dōri de*: with reason; it stands to reason; no wonder.

Yamato: *Kongari yakete irasshaimasu ne. Umi desu ka.*

Wakabayashi: *Ē, Pūketto ni itte kita n' desu. Yakisugite mada hiri-hiri shichatte.*

Yamato: *Ii desu ne. Goshujin to go-issho ni?*

Wakabayashi: *Ē mā.*

Yamato: *Urayamashii wa. Uchi nanka, natsu-yasumi mo kek-kyoku ie de gorogoro shite 'ru dake. Chikagoro buku-buku futotte kichatte. Sore ni shite mo, go-sei ga demasu ne.*

Wakabayashi: *Toraiasuron o yatte iru mono desu kara.*

Yamato: *E––, ano tetsujin-rēsu no? Sugoi wā.*

Wakabayashi: *Sugoku nai n' desu yo. Jogingu kara hajimete, jirijiri to kyori o nobashite itte... Kotsukotsu renshū sureba, dare ni de mo dekimasu yo.*

Yamato: *Jā, Pūketto de mo, torēningu o?*

Wakabayashi: *Mochiron.*

Yamato: *Dōri de surarito shite irassharu to omotta wa. Go-shujin mo yappari?*

Wakabayashi: *Īe, uchi no wa zunguri-mukkuri no jun–Nihon-gata. Gakusei-jidai wa sumō-bu desu mono.*

Yamato: *Mā, gasshiri shite ite ii ja arimasen no. Torēningu ni mo tsukiatte kudasaru n' deshō?*

Wakabayashi: *Masaka. Kinai de wa gussuri, hoteru de wa guttari, umibe de wa gorogoro shite ita dake desu wa.*

☆

Yamato: What a lovely copper tan you have! Did you go to the beach?

Wakabayashi: Yes, I just came back from Phuket (Thailand). I got a sunburn, and it still stings.

Yamato: Wow, Phuket. Did you go with your husband?

Wakabayashi: Well, yes, as a matter of fact.

Yamato: I'm so envious. All my husband does is lie around the house, even during his summer vacation. Lately he's been putting on weight, too. But, hey, you're getting quite a workout.

Wakabayashi: You see, I do triathlons.

Yamato: What, you mean those iron-man races? That's amazing!

Wakabayashi: There's nothing amazing about it. I just started by jogging, and little by little built up to longer distances. Anyone can do it—you just have to keep plugging away.

Yamato: Did you train when you were at Phuket, too?

Wakabayashi: Of course.

Yamato: I *thought* you looked so nice and slim. Your husband's the same, I suppose.

Wakabayashi: Not at all. He's a typical dumpy Japanese guy. In fact, he was on the sumo team in college.

Yamato: Well, it must be nice to have a solid, well-built man. I suppose he goes along when you're training.

Wakabayashi: Ha! That's a laugh. He conked out on the airplane, pooped out at the hotel, and stretched out when we got to the beach.

こんがり (kongari) G

To be burned or toasted to a pleasant, golden brown.

❏ トーストはこんがりきつね色になるまで焼いてね。

Tōsuto wa kongari kitsune-iro ni naru made yaite ne.

Toast the bread until it's a nice, light brown, all right?

❏ 夏はやっぱりこんがりと小麦色に焼けた肌が魅力的だね。

Natsu wa yappari kongari to komugi-iro ni yaketa hada ga miryoku-teki da ne.

A nice, coffee-brown tan really does looks great in summer.

ごろごろ (gorogoro) N / B

(1) The sound or fact of some large, bulky object, animal, or person rolling or tumbling over. *Gorogoro* can also refer to many such objects in confused disarray (N). (2) To spend time doing nothing—includes the image of a person lolling in a recumbent position (N/B).

❏ 引っ越しって本当に大変ね、うちなんかまだダンボールがごろごろ転がったままよ。

Hikkoshi tte hontō ni taihen ne, uchi nanka mada danbōru ga gorogoro korogatta mama yo.

Moving is a real pain. We still have cardboard boxes scattered all over the house.

❑ 「落石注意」と書かれていても、実際にごろごろ岩が落ちてきたら ひとたまりもない*ね。

"Rakuseki chūi" to kakarete ite mo, jissai ni gorogoro iwa ga ochite kitara hito-tamari mo nai ne.

The sign says "Watch for Falling Rocks," but if boulders really started tumbling down, there wouldn't be much you could do (you'd be a goner).

> * *Hito-tamari mo nai*: not be able to withstand something for even a short time (*hito-tamari*, lit. "a single puddle").

❑ 休みの日は思いきり朝寝坊して、一日中家でごろごろしているのが 最高だね。

Yasumi no hi wa omoikiri asa-nebō shite, ichinichi-jū ie de gorogoro shite iru no ga saikō da ne.

My favorite way to spend a day off is to sleep as late as I can in the morning and then spend the rest of the day lounging around the house.

❑ いい若い者が、いつまでごろごろ寝ているんですか。

Ii wakai mono ga, itsu made gorogoro nete iru n' desu ka.

How long do you plan to stay sacked out like this, a healthy young fellow like you?

ぶくぶく (bukubuku) B

Fat, swollen, puffy; said of the human body due to an excess of fat, fluid, or clothing.

❑ 結婚したら急にぶくぶくと太りだしちゃって、みんなに冷やかされ るんです。

Kekkon shitara kyū ni bukubuku to futoridashichatte, minna ni hiya-kasareru n' desu.

Everyone kids me because I plumped out soon after I got married.

❑ 冬のラッシュはいやですね。みんなぶくぶくに着ぶくれ*して身動 きもできません。

Fuyu no rasshu wa iya desu ne. Minna bukubuku ni kibukure shite mi-ugoki mo dekimasen.

I hate the train during rush hour in winter. With all the bulky clothes everyone is wearing, you can hardly move.

> * *Kibukure*: from *kiru* (to wear) and *fukureru* (to swell).

じりじり (jirijiri)　N

(1) To move or advance slowly but steadily in a certain direction. (2) Bright, direct, scorching sunlight.

❑ このところじりじり物価が上がっているから、生活費がかさんで困るわ。

Kono tokoro jirijiri bukka ga agatte iru kara, seikatsu-hi ga kasande komaru wa.

The way prices keep climbing, I'm feeling the pinch in my living expenses.

❑ まだ5月なのに、沖縄は太陽がじりじり照りつけてまるで真夏のようだったよ。

Mada gogatsu na no ni, Okinawa wa taiyō ga jirijiri teritsukete maru de manatsu no yō datta yo.

In Okinawa the sun was beating down so hard that it felt practically like midsummer, though it was still only May.

こつこつ (kotsukotsu)　G

To do something slowly but surely, without flash or ostentation. Often used in a positive sense to describe steady, continuous effort.

❑ 兄はひらめき型、弟はこつこつ型なんだが、僕は困ったことにどっちでもないんだ。

Ani wa hirameki-gata, otōto wa kotsukotsu-gata nan da ga, boku wa komatta koto ni dotchi de mo nai n' da.

My big brother is a real brain, and my little brother is the slow-but-steady type. My problem is that I'm neither one nor the other.

❑ こつこつと勉強するのがどうも苦手で、いつも一夜漬けになっちゃうんです。

Kotsukotsu to benkyō suru no ga dōmo nigate de, itsumo ichiya-zuke ni natchau n' desu.

I'm no good at keeping up with my studies. I always wind up pulling an all-nighter.

すらりと (surarito)　G

Slim, svelte, slender. Often used to describe thin, attractive bodies, arms, legs, etc.

❑ マイケルってかっこいいのよ。すらりと背が高くてね。

Maikeru tte kakko ii no yo. Surarito se ga takakute ne.

Michael is one cool-looking guy. So tall and slender and all.

❑ すらりと伸びた足さえあれば、ミニスカートをはけるんだけど。

Surarito nobita ashi sae areba, mini-sukāto o hakeru n' da kedo.

If my legs were only nice and long and slim, I could wear a miniskirt, too.

ずんぐりむっくり／ずんぐり (zunguri-mukkuri/zunguri)　N / B

Short and fat, dumpy, stout, portly. *Zunguri-mukkuri* is more emphatic.

❑ この大根は、ずんぐりしていて見栄え*は悪いけど、すごくおいしいよ。

Kono daikon wa, zunguri shite ite mibae wa warui kedo, sugoku oishii yo.

This giant radish doesn't look like much, all bloated up the way it is, but it tastes great.

* *Mibae*: outward appearance (positive unless with negative qualifier).

❑ 道産子はサラブレッドと違ってずんぐりむっくりだけど、馬力があるんだよ。

Dosan-ko wa sarabureddo to chigatte zunguri-mukkuri da kedo, bariki ga aru n' da.

Hokkaido-bred horses are much stockier than thoroughbreds, but they've got a lot of power.

がっしり (gasshiri)　G

Strong, solidly built, rugged, muscular.

❑ 男の人はやっぱりがっしりしていないとね。

Otoko no hito wa yappari gasshiri shite inai to ne.

A man's no good if he's not a hunk. (I like a man who's really solidly built.)

❑ 古い家なんですけどがっしりできているんで、まだ壊すにはちょっともったいないんです。

Furui ie nan desu kedo gasshiri dekite iru n' de, mada kowasu ni wa chotto mottainai n' desu.

This house is old but it's as solid as a rock. It would be a shame to tear it down now.

ぐっすり (gussuri)　G / N

To sleep soundly, to be fast asleep.

❑ 夕べはぐっすり寝ていたから、地震があったなんて全然知らなかったなあ。

Yūbe wa gussuri nete ita kara, jishin ga atta nan te zenzen shiranakatta nā.

I was sleeping like a log last night, so I had no idea there was an earthquake.

❏ 風邪薬を飲んでぐっすり眠ったら、頭痛がとれたわ。

Kaze-gusuri o nonde gussuri nemuttara, zutsū ga toreta wa.

I got rid of my headache by taking some cold medicine and getting a good night's sleep.

ぐったり (guttari) B

To be tired, droopy, or desiccated because of fatigue, illness, dehydration, disappointment, etc. Usually used to describe people, animals, or plants.

❏ 田舎に帰ったのはいいけど、まいったよ。帰省*ラッシュで着いた頃にはもうぐったりさ。

Inaka ni kaetta no wa ii kedo, maitta yo. Kisei-rasshu de tsuita koro ni wa mō guttari sa.

It was nice getting back to my hometown again, but the going-home rush was a bitch. By the time I got there I was completely wiped out.

  * *Kisei*: lit., "to return and inquire (as to the health of one's parents)"; to return to one's home outside the big city.

❏ あまりの暑さに、庭の花までぐったりしおれているわ。

Amari no atsusa ni, niwa no hana made guttari shiorete iru wa.

It's so hot, even the flowers in the garden are wilting (going limp).

➥ *Kisei-rasshu* (帰省ラッシュ) refers to the mass movement of people from Tokyo and other big cities back to their hometowns during the Obon and New Year's holiday seasons. Trains and airplanes are packed, and traffic jams on expressways can stretch for a hundred kilometers or more.

The word "Obon" comes from the 盂蘭盆会 *Urabon-e*, or Bon Festival, which is based on the Buddhist text 盂蘭盆経 *Urabon-kyō*, or *Ullambana Sutra*. The original purpose of the festival was to comfort the spirits of the dead, and in fact many Japanese still choose this occasion to visit the graves of their ancestors. Less ghostly customs have become associated with the festival as well, including 盆踊り *bon odori*, the folk dances performed in the summer evening in nearly every town, village, and neighborhood in Japan. Obon is celebrated in mid-July in some areas and mid-August in others, but the peak of the *kisei-rasshu* comes around August 15, and stores often close for a few days then. A similar rush to the countryside to visit relatives occurs at New Year's, for most people have at least January 1, 2, and 3 as holidays.

A Big Headache

Makoto Saitō, an employee of Taishō Bank, has been drowsy all morning. His coworker Shigeo Suzuki detects evidence of a hangover.

A Big Headache

鈴木　「うかない*顔ですね。」

斉藤　「いやあ†、まいりました。」

鈴木　（手で口元にお猪口を持っていく動作をして）「コレですか。」

斉藤　「支店長とね。朝起きたら、頭は**がんがん**、胃は**むかむか**。」

鈴木　「つらいですよね。」

斉藤　「起き上がろうとしたら、もう**くらくら**しちゃって。」

鈴木　「わかります、わかります。そういうときに、会議で**くどくど**部長のお説教を聞かされると、こたえるんですよね。」

斉藤　「**げんなり**ですね。しかし、夕べは変だなあ。**べろべろ**になるまで飲んだわけでもないのに。年かなあ。」

鈴木　「普段**ばりばり**やっている分、ストレスがたまってたんじゃないですか。」

斉藤　「支店長も**ぐいぐい**コップ酒でいっちゃって。最後にはカウンターで**うつらうつら**ですよ。」

鈴木　「それじゃあ、支店長を送っていったんですか。」

斉藤　「そうそう。何しろ❖**たっぷり**1時間は乗りますからね。ぼくもタクシーの中でつい✿**うとうと**しちゃって。」

鈴木　「大変でしたね。」

斉藤　「ええ、まあ。あっ、大変だ。」

鈴木　「何ですか、急に。」

斉藤　「**うっかり**タクシー代の領収書をもらうのを忘れた！」

---

* *Ukanai*: lit., not floating; downcast, crestfallen.

† *Iyā*: an exclamation expressing surprise, embarrassment, etc.

❖ *Nani shiro*: in any case, anyhow; emphasizing what follows.

✿ *Tsui*: in the end, before realizing it.

Suzuki: *Ukanai kao desu ne.*

Saitō: *Iyā, mairimashita.*

Suzuki: *(te de kuchimoto ni ochoko o motte iku dōsa o shite):* Kore desu ka.

Saitō: *Shiten-chō to ne. Asa okitara, atama wa gangan, i wa muka-muka.*

Suzuki: *Tsurai desu yo ne.*

Saitō: *Okiagarō to shitara, mō kurakura shichatte.*

Suzuki: *Wakarimasu, wakarimasu. Sō iu toki ni, kaigi de kudokudo buchō no osekkyō o kikasareru to, kotaeru n' desu yo ne.*

Saitō: *Gennari desu ne. Shikashi, yūbe wa hen da nā. Berobero ni naru made nonda wake de mo nai no ni. Toshi ka nā.*

Suzuki: *Fudan baribari yatte iru bun, sutoresu ga tamatte 'ta n' ja nai desu ka.*

Saitō: *Shiten-chō mo guigui koppu-zake de itchatte. Saigo ni wa kauntā de utsura-utsura desu yo.*

Suzuki: *Sore jā, shiten-chō o okutte itta n' desu ka.*

Saitō: *Sō sō. Nani shiro tappuri ichi-jikan wa norimasu kara ne. Boku mo takushī no naka de tsui utouto shichatte.*

Suzuki: *Taihen deshita ne.*

Saitō: *Ē, mā. A—, taihen da.*

Suzuki: *Nan desu ka, kyū ni.*

Saitō: *Ukkari takushī-dai no ryōshū-sho o morau no o wasureta!*

★

Suzuki: You really look down in the dumps today.

Saitō: Yeah, it's the pits all right.

Suzuki: (cupping one hand and raising it to his mouth as if to drink from a sake cup) Is this the problem?

Saitō: Yeah, I was out with the branch manager. This morning I woke up to a pounding headache and a churning stomach.

Suzuki: That's too bad.

Saitō: When I tried to get up, I felt sort of woozy.

Suzuki: I know what you mean. And then if you've got to listen to the division chief give one of his sermons at a meeting, it can be pretty tough.

Saitō: Yeah, I'm sick of it. Last night was funny, though. I didn't drink myself under the table or anything. Maybe I'm getting old.

Suzuki: You always put so much into your work (work your tail off), maybe the stress is getting to you.

Saitō: The branch manager was drinking sake from a glass and really guzzling it down. Near the end he nodded off right there at the counter.

Suzuki: So you had to see him home?

Saitō: That's right. Anyhow, it took a solid hour to get home. I ended up conking out (nodding off) in the cab myself.

Suzuki: Sounds tough.

Saitō: Yeah, well…. Oh-oh, now I've blown it.

Suzuki: What's the matter?

Saitō: The taxi fare! I completely forgot to get a receipt.

➡ Sake is usually poured from a small earthenware bottle called a 徳利 *tokkuri* into a small cup called an お猪口 *ochoko* or 杯 *sakazuki* or into a slightly larger vessel called a ぐい飲み *guinomi*. The cupping of the right hand as if holding a *tokkuri* and bringing it near the mouth is simple sign language for drinking sake.

While drinkers usually sip sake slowly from a *tokkuri* or *guinomi*, when they want to proceed at a fast pace they drink from a small glass called a コップ *koppu*, hence コップ酒 *koppu-zake* (often sold in vending machines in a small cuplike bottle). (Note that *koppu*, taken from the Dutch word *kop*, means "a glass," while カップ *kappu*, from the English "cup," means just that: "a cup.")

むかむか (mukamuka) B

To feel woozy, nauseous. Or to be so discomforted, angry, etc. that you feel like throwing up.

❏ 乗り物酔いかしら、なんだかむかむかしてきたわ。

Norimono-yoi kashira, nan da ka mukamuka shite kita wa.

Maybe I'm getting carsick. I think I'm going to throw up.

❏ きのうの課長の言い草、思い出しただけでもむかむかするね。

Kinō no kachō no iigusa, omoidashita dake de mo mukamuka suru ne.

Just thinking about the way the section chief talked yesterday is enough to make you puke (make you sick to your stomach).

くらくら (kurakura) N

To feel dizzy, shaky, unsteady on one's feet.

❏ 頭がくらくらするんだけど、血圧でも高いのかしら。

Atama ga kurakura suru n' da kedo, ketsuatsu de mo takai no kashira.

My head seems to be spinning. I wonder if I might have high blood pressure or something.

❏ 転勤を言いわたされたときには、一瞬*くらくらきたよ。

Tenkin o iiwatasareta toki ni wa, isshun kurakura kita yo.

When they told me I was going to be transferred, you could have knocked me over with a feather.

   * *Isshun*: (for) an instant.

くどくど (kudokudo) B

To say the same thing over and over again. Often used to describe annoying long-windedness.

❏ くどくどと言い訳したところで、物事何も進展しないよ。

Kudokudo to iiwake shita tokoro de, monogoto nani mo shinten shinai yo.

Nothing is going to be accomplished by your going on and on making excuses.

❏ 年のせい*か母も愚痴っぽくなって†ね、会うたびにくどくど聞かされるんで弱っちゃう◆よ。

Toshi no sei ka haha mo guchippoku natte ne, au tabi ni kudokudo kikasareru n' de yowatchau yo.

My mother's really turned into a complainer in her old age. Every time I see her, she nearly talks me to death.

   * *Sei*: on account of.
   † *Guchippoi*: complaining (*guchi* "complaints" + the adjective-forming *ppoi*).
   ◆ *Yowaru*: lit., weakened; at a loss, flummoxed.

げんなり (gennari) B

To feel exhausted, beat, worn out, burned out, disgusted. While *unzari* expresses mental exhaustion or disgust, *gennari* describes a lack of energy that is both mental and physical.

❏ けさったら*、事故で 2 時間も満員電車に閉じ込められたんだぜ。
もううんざりだよ。

*Kesa ttara, jiko de ni-jikan mo man'in-densha ni tojikomerareta n' da ze.
Mō gennari da yo.*

This morning—would you believe it—there was this accident, and I was
trapped in a crowded train for two solid hours. I've had it up to here.

　　* *Ttara*: introduces a subject with a modicum of criticism, denigration, or
　　 intimacy. Used in a colloquial context.

❏ 決算期にはくる日もくる日も数字とにらめっこ*で、いいかげん†げ
んなりするよ。

*Kessan-ki ni wa kuru hi mo kuru hi mo sūji to niramekko de, ii kagen
gennari suru yo.*

When we're closing the books, I spend day after day staring at numbers.
I'm fed up with it.

　　* *Niramekko*: outstaring or staring down.
　　† *Ii kagen*: originally, the proper amount or degree; here, colloquial for
　　 "pretty much, considerably."

ぺろぺろ (berobero) B

(1) To stick out one's tongue in an exaggerated manner and lick
something repeatedly. (2) To be drunk to the point of physical im-
pairment.

❏ 犬に顔をぺろぺろなめられて、くすぐったかったわ。

Inu ni kao o berobero namerarete, kusuguttakatta wa.

This dog licked me all over the face. My, did it tickle!

❏ 夕べはぺろぺろに酔っぱらって帰ってきたけど、何かいやなことで
もあったの。

*Yūbe wa berobero ni yopparatte kaette kita kedo, nani ka iya na koto de
mo atta no.*

You were drunk as a skunk when you got home last night. What was the
matter?

ばりばり (baribari) G / N

(1) The sound of something being ripped, torn, scratched, struck, or
crunched (N). (2) To do something steadily, energetically. Often
used to describe a person who works hard and enthusiastically (G/N).
(3) Stiff, rigid (N).

❏ ごませんべいをばりばり食べながら、相撲をテレビで見るのが土日
の楽しみなんだ。

Goma-senbei o baribari tabenagara, sumō o terebi de miru no ga do-nichi no tanoshimi nan da.

Munching on sesame crackers while watching sumo on TV—that's how I like to spend my weekends.

❏ あいかわらず、彼女はばりばり仕事をしているよ。

Aikawarazu, kanojo wa baribari shigoto o shite iru yo.

She's still going hot and heavy at her work. Hasn't changed one bit.

❏ 寺沢さんは、現役*ばりばりの政治記者だから、お忙しいんじゃないですか。

Terasawa-san wa, gen'eki baribari no seiji-kisha da kara, oisogashii n' ja nai desu ka.

As a political journalist at the peak of his career, Mr. Terasawa must be terribly busy.

 * *Gen'eki*: on active duty; active (not retired or out of the mainstream).

❏ タオルを外に干しておいたら、ばりばりに凍っちゃったわ。

Taoru o soto ni hoshite oitara, baribari ni kōtchatta wa.

The towels froze and got all crackly when I hung them out to dry.

➡ *Sembei* are roasted crackers made from rice or wheat flower and flavored with soy sauce, salt, sugar, and other ingredients. *Goma sembei* contain soy sauce and sesame seeds.

While sumo ranks a distant second to baseball among spectator sports in Japan, it does enjoy a steady popularity. Six fifteen-day tournaments are held each year, and all are broadcast by NHK, the public television and radio network.

ぐいぐい (guigui) G / N

(1) To drink sake or another liquid quickly and vigorously. The word is used positively to denote a lively, enthusiastic style of drinking. (2) To push or pull strongly or steadily. To do something with energy or vigor.

❏ 夏は冷えたビールをぐいぐい飲むのが最高ですね。

Natsu wa hieta bīru o guigui nomu no ga saikō desu ne.

When summer comes around, there's nothing like chugging down (wetting your whistle with) a nice cold beer or two.

❏ やっぱり男の人は、ぐいぐい引っ張ってくれるような人が頼もしくていいわ。

Yappari otoko no hito wa, guigui hippatte kureru yō na hito ga tonomoshikute ii wa.

After all is said and done, give me a strong man who takes the lead.

うつらうつら (utsura-utsura) N

To doze off. To drift back and forth between light sleep and drowsy wakefulness.

❑ 陽当たりのいい席だと、つい午後の授業はうつらうつらしてしまうんです。

Hiatari no ii seki da to, tsui gogo no jugyō wa utsura-utsura shite shimau n' desu.

If I get a seat in the sun during an afternoon class, I wind up nodding off.

❑ 目覚まし時計のベルを止めてから、ほんのちょっとうつらうつらするのが気持ちいいよね。

Mezamashi-dokei no beru o tomete kara, hon no chotto utsura-utsura suru no ga kimochi ii yo ne.

Switching off the alarm clock and then dozing off for a few more winks just can't be beat.

たっぷり (tappuri) G / N

Full, complete, more than sufficient, replete. Often used after a noun, as in 皮肉たっぷり *hiniku-tappuri* "awfully sarcastic," and 愛嬌たっぷり *aikyō-tappuri* "loaded with charm." When used before or after a numerical quantity, *tappuri* indicates that the quantity is met fully or even exceeded, as shown by the dialogue for this chapter.

❑ さっき*の課長の発言、いやみたっぷりだったと思いませんか。

Sakki no kachō no hatsugen, iyami tappuri datta to omoimasen ka.

Didn't you think that what the section chief said a while ago was just dripping with sarcasm?

* *Sakki*: colloquial version of *saki* (previous, earlier).

❑ 上着はむしろたっぷりしたものを選んだ方がきれいに着こなせます。

Uwagi wa mushiro tappuri shita mono o eranda hō ga kirei ni kikonase-masu.

I think you would look much better if you chose a looser fitting jacket.

うとうと (utouto) N

To fall into a light sleep. Used when one has fallen asleep without realizing it because of sickness or exhaustion.

❑ こたつに入ってテレビを見ているうちに、ついうとうととしちゃったわ。

Kotatsu ni haitte terebi o mite iru uchi ni, tsui utouto shichatta wa.

I was sitting in the *kotatsu* and watching TV, when before I knew it I had nodded off to sleep.

❑ いい気持ちでうとうとしていたのに、電話がかかってきてたたき起こされちゃった*よ。

Ii kimochi de utouto shite ita no ni, denwa ga kakatte kite tataki-okosarechatta yo.

I was just floating off into dreamland when the goddamn telephone rang and woke me up.

　* *Tatakiokosu*: rouse, roust, wake up.

➥ The *kotatsu* is a traditional Japanese heating device. In its original form, a small charcoal brazier is placed inside a square hole cut into the tatami or floor, and a small frame covered with a futon is put over the hole. To get warm, you stick your legs into the hole and wrap the edge of the futon around yourself. This is called a *horigotatsu*. These days, most kotasu look like low, square tables that are placed directly on the tatami or carpet. An electric heater under the tabletop provides the warmth. While *horigotatsu* are more comfortable since you can let your legs dangle down, electric *kotatsu* are more convenient because you don't have to light the coals and there's no danger of carbon monoxide poisoning. For many Japanese, the ultimate in family togetherness during the winter is to sit snug and warm in the *kotatsu* while eating *mikan* (mandarin oranges).

うっかり (ukkari) B

To forget, miss, or fail to pay attention to something important.

❑ うっかりしてたなあ。きょう彼女と約束してたんだ。

Ukkari shite 'ta nā. Kyō kanojo to yakusoku shite 'ta n' da.

Darn it! I had a date with my girlfriend today and it completely slipped my mind.

❑ ごめんなさいね、酔っ払ってついうっかり口をすべらせちゃったのよ。

Gomen nasai ne, yopparatte tsui ukkari kuchi o suberasechatta no yo.

I'm really sorry. The liquor went to my head and it just slipped out.

Feeling Out of Sorts?

TARO

Masaru Kodera, who works at the Nippon Real Estate Co., is feeling out of sorts, so he's gone to a clinic for a check-up. Dr. Akio Kadota, a specialist in internal medicine, is now examining him.

Feeling Out of Sorts?

門田　「どうしました？」

小寺　「どうも風邪をこじらせたみたいで。最初はのどが**ひりひり**する程度だったんですけど、そのうちせきも出るようになって、夜中にのどが**ぜいぜい**するんです。」

門田　「どんなせきが出ますか。**こんこん**とか、**ごほんごほん**とか……。」

小寺　「**ごほんごほん**という感じですね。」

門田　「熱はありますか。」

小寺　「はい、きのうから。夕べは**ぞくぞく**寒気がしたので、高熱が出るんじゃないかと**ひやひや**したんですが、今のところ*7度8分くらいでおさまっています。」

門田　「食欲はどうですか。」

小寺　「**もりもり**というわけにはいきませんが、まあまああります。あと、目が**しょぼしょぼ**して頭も重いんです。」

門田　「他には？」

小寺　「胃が**しくしく**痛むことがあります。それと、あのう……。実は、先生、どうしても会社に行きたくないんです。」

Ima no tokoro: at present, for the moment.

Kadota: *Dō shimashita?*

Kodera: *Dōmo kaze o kojiraseta mitai de. Saisho wa nodo ga hiri-hiri suru teido datta n' desu kedo, sono uchi seki mo deru yō ni natte, yonaka ni nodo ga zeizei suru n' desu.*

Kadota: *Donna seki ga demasu ka. Konkon to ka, gohongohon to ka...*

Kodera: *Gohongohon to iu kanji desu ne.*

Kadota: *Netsu wa arimasu ka.*

Kodera: *Hai, kinō kara. Yūbe wa zokuzoku samuke ga shita no de, kōnetsu ga deru n' ja nai ka to hiyahiya shita n' desu ga, ima no tokoro nana-do hachi-bu kurai de osamatte imasu.*

Kadota: *Shokuyoku wa dō desu ka.*

Kodera: *Morimori to iu wake ni wa ikimasen ga, māmā arimasu. Ato, me ga shoboshobo shite atama mo omoi n' desu.*

Kadota: *Hoka ni wa?*

Kodera: *I ga shikushiku itamu koto ga arimasu. Sore to, anō... Jitsu wa, sensei, dōshite mo kaisha ni ikitaku nai n' desu.*

☆

Kadota: So what's the problem?

Kodera: I think I've aggravated a cold. At first my throat was just a little prickly, but then I started coughing. Late at night I get all wheezy.

Kadota: What kind of cough is it? Just a regular cough, or are you really hacking?

Kodera: More like hacking.

Kadota: Do you have a fever?

Kodera: Yes, I do, since yesterday. Last night I came down with the chills and started shivering, and I was afraid I'd get a really high fever. Now it's only about 37.8° C [100° F], though.

Kadota: Do you have much of an appetite?

Kodera: I'm not exactly shoveling it down, but I'm eating all right. Other than that, my eyes are sort of watery, and my head feels like a ton of bricks.

Kadota: Anything else?

Kodera: Sometimes I get this dull pain in my stomach, and, um, uh … To tell you the truth, Doc, I just don't feel like going to work.

ひりひり (hirihiri) N / B

A feeling of continuous pain or irritation on the skin, inside the mouth or nose, etc.

❑ どうも背中がひりひりすると思ったら、日焼けで水ぶくれができていたんです。

Dōmo senaka ga hirihiri suru to omottara, hiyake de mizubukure ga dekite ita n' desu.

I had this funny stinging feeling on my back, and what should it be but blisters from my sunburn.

❑ タイ料理はうまいですね。ひりひりする辛さが、こたえられません*よ。

Tai-ryōri wa umai desu ne. Hirihiri suru karasa ga, kotaeraremasen yo.

Thai food sure is good. I love the tingling feeling the spices give you.

   * *Kotaeru*: to bear, endure; in the negative, can't bear something (because it is so good).

ぜいぜい (zeizei) N / B

The sound or feeling of air being forced through the windpipe when you have a cold or other respiratory illness.

❑ そんなにぜいぜいしているんなら、医者に診てもらった方がいいんじゃないですか。

Sonna ni zeizei shite iru n' nara, isha ni mite moratta hō ga ii n' ja nai desu ka.

With a wheeze like that, don't you think you should have a doctor take a look at you?

❑ ぜん息は怖いですよ。発作が起こるとぜいぜいして死ぬかと思いますよ。

Zensoku wa kowai desu yo. Hossa ga okoru to zeizei shite shinu ka to omoimasu yo.

Asthma is really scary. When I get an attack, I feel like I'm going to wheeze myself to death.

こんこん (konkon)　N / B

A light cough. Small children use this word to describe coughing in general.

❏ 明け方になるとこんこんせきが出て、目が覚めるんです。

Akegata ni naru to konkon seki ga dete, me ga sameru n' desu.

Around dawn I start coughing and it wakes me up.

❏ こんこんが出るから、暖かくして早く寝なさい。

Konkon ga deru kara, atatakaku shite hayaku nenasai.

You'll get a cough, so make yourself warm and go right to bed. (to a child)

ごほんごほん (gohongohon)　N / B

The sound of a loud, heavy cough from deep in the throat or any wet, phlegmy cough.

❏ 人の顔に向かってごほんごほんとせきをするなんて、失礼ね。

Hito no kao ni mukatte gohongohon to seki o suru nante, shitsurei ne.

It's so rude to let loose with a hacking cough right in someone's face like that.

❏ 課長ったら、ごほんごほんとせき込みながらもタバコを離さないのよ。どうか*と思うわ。

Kachō ttara, gohongohon to sekikominagara mo tabako o hanasanai no yo. Dōka to omou wa.

The section chief is really something. He keeps on smoking even when he's coughing his head off. I can't believe it!

* *Dōka*: expresses wonder or perplexity at some uncommon situation.

ぞくぞく (zokuzoku)　G / N / B

Shivering with cold (N/B) or with pleasure, expectation, nervousness, fear, etc. (G/N/B).

❏ 何だか*背すじがぞくぞくするんです。熱が上がりそうなので早退させてください。

Nan da ka sesuji ga zokuzoku suru n' desu. Netsu ga agarisō na no de sōtai sasete kudasai.

I'm getting chills up and down my back, and I think my temperature is going up. Is it all right if I leave early?

* *Nan da ka*: for some reason or other.

❏ このミステリーはおもしろいよ。ぞくぞくするほどスリリングなんだ。

Kono misuterī wa omoshiroi yo. Zokuzoku suru hodo suriringu nan da.

This mystery is really great. It's so thrilling it gives me the chills.

ひやひや (hiyahiya) B

The feeling of fear or worry in a dangerous situation. Originally a cold or chilly feeling.

❏ やっぱりうそなんかつくもんじゃないなあ。いつばれる*かとひや ひやしたよ。

Yappari uso nanka tsuku mon ja nai nā. Itsu bareru ka to hiyahiya shita yo.

Lying just isn't worth it, after all. I was scared stiff that I'd get caught any minute.

  * *Bareru*: to come into the open.

❏ 彼の車に乗るのはひやひやものよ。飲むわとばすわ*で、命がいく つあっても足りない†わ。

Kare no kuruma ni noru no wa hiyahiya-mono yo. Nomu wa tobasu wa de, inochi ga ikutsu atte mo tarinai wa.

Riding with him is enough to make your hair curl. The way he drinks and burns up the road, it gives you the feeling you're living on borrowed time.

  * *... wa ... wa*: doing both one thing and the other.
  † *Inochi ga ikutsu atte mo tarinai*: lit., no matter how many lives one had, they wouldn't be enough.

もりもり (morimori) G

To be full, strong, powerful. By extension, to be very hungry, eager, peppy. The word also describes an action that is performed vigorously, enthusiastically, energetically.

❏ 堀田さんはボディビルをやっているだけあって、筋肉もりもりだよ。

Hotta-san wa bodībiru o yatte iru dake atte, kinniku morimori da yo.

The way Hotta has been hitting the weights, it's no wonder his muscles are practically popping (bulging) out of his skin.

❏ もりもり食べるだけじゃなくて、もりもり働いてほしいもんだね。

Morimori taberu dake ja nakute, morimori hataraite hoshii mon da ne.

I wish he wouldn't just eat like a horse but would work like one, too.

しょぼしょぼ (shoboshobo) B

(1) To have bleary, sleepy, or squinty eyes. (2) A continuous gloomy

drizzle; getting wet and feeling miserable in such weather. (3) A listless, lackluster feeling.

❑ 夕べ日本語の擬音語・擬態語についての本を読みだしたらやめられなくなってね、おかげで*今日は目がしょぼしょぼだよ。

Yūbe Nihon-go no gion-go–gitai-go ni tsuite no hon o yomidashitara yamerarenaku natte ne, okage de kyō wa me ga shoboshobo da yo.

Last night I started reading a book on Japanese onomotopoeia and mimesis, and I just couldn't put it down. That's why my eyes are all puffy today.

　　* *Okage de*: thanks to (that).

❑ 雨がしょぼしょぼ降っていると、どうも買い物に出るのがおっくうになるわね。

Ame ga shoboshobo futte iru to, dōmo kaimono ni deru no ga okkū ni naru wa ne.

When it's drizzly out, it's too much of a bother to go out shopping, isn't it.

❑ やっぱり年かなあ、おやじの後ろ姿が何とも*しょぼしょぼしているんだよ。

Yappari toshi ka nā, oyaji no ushirosugata ga nan to mo shoboshobo shite iru n' da yo.

Dad's getting on, I guess. Seen from behind, he just seems to be doddering along.

　　* *Nan to mo*: inexpressably.

しくしく (shikushiku)　N / B

(1) A pain that is sharp and continuous but not too strong (B). (2) Prolonged sniveling, whimpering, sniffling (N).

❑ 虫歯*がしくしく痛んで夕べは眠れませんでした。

Mushiba ga shikushiku itande yūbe wa nemuremasen deshita.

I couldn't sleep last night because this toothache just wouldn't let up.

　　* *Mushiba*: cavity, dental caries.

❑ 道端でしくしく泣いている女の子がいるから誰かと思ったら、美雪ちゃんじゃないの。

Michibata de shikushiku naite iru onna no ko ga iru kara dare ka to omottara, Miyuki-chan ja nai no.

I was wondering who the little girl sniffling beside the road was, and who should it be but little Miyuki!

➡ Unless you're speaking to a very close friend or relative, you need to tack a suffix onto the name of the person you're talking to. The choice of a suffix reflects the formality of the occasion, the psychological distance between you and the other person, and where you stand relative to him or her in the social hierarchy.

-San ~ さん is the most common, of course. It is found in all kinds of situations, uttered by both men and women, young and old. For very formal occasions or when being very polite to a social superior, you might opt for ~様 *-sama*, but be sure to accompany it with the proper honorific, humble, and polite forms, or whatever you can muster in that regard. In day-to-day life, you're most likely to hear *-sama* used by tellers in banks or clerks in department stores to address their customers.

When you're speaking to a close friend or colleague who's at the same or a lower level in rank, you might want to use ~ちゃん *-chan* or ~くん *-kun* (also written 君) after the first (especially with *-chan*) or the last name, the former most often in reference to women, the latter to men. When *-chan* is used after the full last name, however, it can leave an impression of courseness. The level of speech should reflect the implied intimacy. (*-Chan* is also the most common suffix for talking to or about babies and children, especially girls; *-kun* is frequently used for boys.)

When two Japanese speakers meet each other for the first time, they have to size each other up to determine what kind of language to use. The important factors include age, social group, job, rank, and accomplishments, and a mistake can be embarrassing. This helps to explain the popularity of business cards: they let people pigeonhole each other at a glance.

The Trials of Middle Managers

TARO

Yoshihide Kakinuma and Yūji Seki are managers at Sakura Publishing Company. Here they are having lunch together in the company cafeteria.

The Trials of Middle Managers

柿沼 「最近の新入社員には**やきもき**させられますよ。」

関 「同感ですね。」

柿沼 **「やんわり**指示すると何にもしない。かといって*、**ば
しっと**言うと**ぶうっと**ふくれる。」

関 「やはり子供の少ない時代で甘やかされて育ったからで
しょうか。手取り足取り†言わないと、ただ**ぼけっと**し
ている、といった感じですね。」

柿沼 「かと思うと❖、ふだん**ぼそぼそ**しゃべるくせに、カラ
オケに行くと人が変わったようにマイクを離さなかっ
たりして。」

関 「どういうんでしょうね。この間も、あんまり**ぐずぐず**
しているんで急がせたら、**ぶすっと**したかと思うと、
目に涙をためているんですよ。」

柿沼 **「めそめそ**されるとこっちも困るし、言い方が難しいで
すね。」

関 「全くです。会社でめそめそ、家で**ぎゃあぎゃあ**……泣
きたいのはこっちの方ですよ。」

---

* *Ka to itte*: used to introduce a contrary or additional comment; similar to "having said that."

† *Tetori-ashitori*: lit., "taking hand, taking foot"; to take someone by the hand and show how to do something.

❖ *Ka to omou to*: indicating successive actions (e.g., "and at the same time"), in this case the preceding and succeeding sentences.

Kakinuma: *Saikin no shinnyū-shain ni wa yakimoki saseraremasu yo.*

Seki: *Dōkan desu ne.*

Kakinuma: *Yanwari shiji suru to nanni mo shinai. Ka to itte, bashitto iu to pūtto fukureru.*

Seki: *Yahari kodomo no sukunai jidai de amayakasarete sodatta kara deshō ka. Tetori-ashitori iwanai to, tada boketto shite iru, to itta kanji desu ne.*

Kakinuma: *Ka to omou to, fudan bosoboso shaberu kuse ni, karaoke ni iku to hito ga kawatta yō ni maiku o hanasanakattari shite.*

Seki: *Dō iu n' deshō ne. Kono aida mo, anmari guzuguzu shite iru n' de isogasetara, busutto shita ka to omou to, me ni namida o tamete iru n' desu yo.*

Kakinuma: *Mesomeso sareru to kotchi mo komaru shi, iikata ga muzukashii desu ne.*

Seki: *Mattaku desu. Kaisha de mesomeso, ie de gyāgyā... Nakitai no wa kotchi no hō desu yo.*

☆

Kakinuma: The new employees these days really keep you guessing.

Seki: I feel the same way.

Kakinuma: If I tell them to do something nicely, they don't do anything at all. Then if I lay down the law, they start pouting.

Seki: What with smaller families these days, maybe they're all growing up spoiled. If you don't spell everything out, they just sit there with their eyes glazed over.

Kakinuma: On the other hand, while they just mumble under their breath most of the time, their whole personality changes when they go to a karaoke. Then they won't let go of the mike.

Seki: How can you explain it? The other day one of them was taking her own sweet time with her work, so I hurried her up a bit. No sooner had she gotten all bent out of shape than her eyes filled up with tears.

Kakinuma: I hate it when they start whining. It's hard to know what to say.

Seki: You're absolutely right. With the employees whining at us at the office and the wife and kids raising a ruckus at home, we're the ones who should be crying.

やきもき (yakimoki) B

To fret, fuss, worry, feel anxious.

❑ いくら周りがやきもきしても、本人がやる気を起こさなければ大学には合格しないよ。

Ikura mawari ga yakimoki shite mo, honnin ga yaru ki o okosanakereba daigaku ni wa gōkaku shinai yo.

It doesn't matter how much the people around him bite their nails. If he doesn't get his act together, he'll never get into college.

❑ ひどい渋滞に巻きこまれちゃって、結婚式に間に合わないんじゃないかとやきもきしたわ。

Hidoi jūtai ni makikomarechatte, kekkon-shiki ni ma ni awanai n' ja nai ka to yakimoki shita wa.

We got stuck in a terrible traffic jam. I was afraid we'd be late for the wedding.

やんわり (yanwari) N

Softly, gently. Describes polite or indirect expressions that are used to soften criticisms, reprimands, etc.

❑ 社会に出たら、相手のいやみをやんわり受け流せるくらいのゆとりはほしいね。

Shakai ni detara, aite no iyami o yanwari ukenagaseru kurai no yutori wa hoshii ne.

Once you get out of school and start working in the real world, you should be flexible (big-minded) enough to shrug off the mean little things people say.

❑ そんなことでどなりつけなくて*も、やんわりと言って聞かせればわかるんですよ。

Sonna koto de donaritsukenakute mo, yanwari to itte kikasereba wakaru n' desu yo.

There's no need to yell like that. Just speak softly and he'll get the point.

* *Donaritsukeru*: to yell at, scream at.

ばしっと (bashitto) N

(1) The cracking sound of dry wood or another hard, thick object splitting, breaking, or hitting something. (2) Actions or words that are firm, unyielding, decisive, adamant.

❏ 打った瞬間ばしっと音がしたと思ったら*、ラケットが折れちゃってね、カッコわるかったよ。

Utta shunkan bashitto oto ga shita to omottara, raketto ga orechatte ne, kakko warukatta yo.

I heard a cracking sound the instant I hit the ball—my racket had broken in two. Boy, did I look stupid.

> ** To omottara*: almost as soon as something comes to awareness, another event occurs; when, as soon as, at the moment of.

❏ あんまりしつこく誘われるから、ばしっと断っちゃったわ。

Anmari shitsukoku sasowareru kara, bashitto kotowatchatta wa.

He made such a nuisance of himself asking me out that I finally turned him down flat.

ぷうっと (pūtto) N / B

(1) A sudden blast or honk from a horn, trumpet, etc., or a snorting sound emitted from the mouth or another bodily orifice. Also used to describe unsuccessfully suppressed laughter (N). (2) An object being inflated quickly (N). (3) A pouty expression of discontent—lower lip distended, cheeks puffed out, etc (B).

❏ この辺は、夕方になるとぷうっとラッパをふきながらお豆腐屋さんが回ってくるのよ。

Kono hen wa, yūgata ni naru to pūtto rappa o fukinagara otōfuya-san ga mawatte kuru no yo.

Every evening, a tofu seller comes by here tooting on a horn.

❏ あまりのおかしさに、思わずぷうっと吹き出しちゃった。

Amari no okashisa ni, omowazu pūtto fukidashichatta.

It was so funny I couldn't help but burst out laughing.

❏ このおもち、そろそろ食べ頃よ。焼けてぷうっとふくれてきたもの。

Kono omochi, sorosoro tabegoro yo. Yakete pūtto fukurete kita mono.

It's about time to eat this mochi. It's all big and puffy now.

❏ 気に入らないとすぐぷうっとふくれるんじゃ、まるで*子供と同じじゃないか。

Ki ni iranai to sugu pūtto fukureru n' ja, maru de kodomo to onaji ja nai ka.

You're just like a little kid, the way you start pouting (get grumpy) whenever you don't like something.

Maru de: exactly like.

➥ *Mochi* is a kind of thick, sticky paste made from a special kind of rice that has been steamed, kneaded, and shaped into a round or square cake. Eaten either raw or cooked, it is often a special treat at New Year's and during celebrations. Cooked, it swells slightly.

ぼけっと (boketto) N / B

To gaze vacantly off into space, without thinking or doing anything (N/B). Used critically of someone who sits around and doesn't notice work that needs to be done (B).

❑ たまには海でも見ながら、一日中ぼけっとして過ごしたいなあ。

Tama ni wa umi de mo minagara, ichinichi-jū boketto shite sugoshitai nā.

Sometimes I just want to spend the whole day taking it easy, gazing at the ocean or something.

❑ 何をぼけっとそんなところで突っ立ってるんだ、危ないじゃないか。

Nani o boketto sonna tokoro de tsuttatte 'ru n' da, abunai ja nai ka.

What are you doing standing there like a goddam telephone pole? Don't you know it's dangerous?

ぼそぼそ (bosoboso) B

(1) Spoken in a hushed, unclear voice. (2) Of food: dry, tasteless, unappetizing.

❑ あの人、いつもぼそぼそと話して何となく陰気な感じね。

Ano hito, itsumo bosoboso to hanashite nan to naku inki na kanji ne.

There's something spooky about that fellow, the way he talks under his breath all the time.

❑ ご飯に麦を混ぜると、体にはいいかもしれないけど、何だかぼそぼそするわね。

Gohan ni mugi o mazeru to, karada ni wa ii kamo shirenai kedo, nan da ka bosoboso suru wa ne.

Rice mixed with barley might be good for your health, but somehow it tastes like sawdust.

➥ Rice is the staple food of Japan, of course, particularly white rice that is boiled and served without any flavoring. Starchy, sticky rice is especially prized, with varieties like *sasanishiki* and *koshihikari* fetching high prices for their agglutinating texture.

ぐずぐず (guzuguzu) B

(1) To stretch out a job, vacillate, procrastinate, waste time. (2) Used to describe a whiny, fussy, demanding child or a grumbling, complaining adult who acts like a child. (3) Of clothing etc.: loose, baggy, unshapen. (4) The sound or feeling a stuffy nose.

❑ ぐずぐずしていると学校に遅れますよ。

Guzuguzu shite iru to gakkō ni okuremasu yo.

If you keep dawdling (fooling around), you're going to be late for school.

❑ 何をぐずぐずしているんだ。さっさととりかかりなさい。

Nani o guzuguzu shite iru n' da. Sassa to torikakarinasai.

What are you dragging your feet for? Get cracking!

❑ 子供じゃあるまいし*、いつまでぐずぐず言っているんだ。

Kodomo ja aru mai shi, itsu made guzuguzu itte iru n' da.

You aren't a young kid, for God's sake. How long are you going to keep fussing? (Grow up and stop whining like a baby!)

  * *Ja aru mai shi*: in spite of the fact that you are not *something*, with strong critical overtones.

❑ 着付けがうまくないもんだから、帯がぐずぐずにゆるんじゃったわ。

Kitsuke ga umaku nai mon da kara, obi ga guzuguzu ni yurunjatta wa.

My obi wasn't tied properly, so now it's coming loose.

❑ 毎年この季節になると、花粉症で鼻がぐずぐずするわ、頭は重いわで憂うつなんですよ。

Mai-nen kono kisetsu ni naru to, kafun-shō de hana ga guzuguzu suru wa, atama wa omoi wa de yūutsu nan desu yo.

Every year about this time, I get the sniffles from hay fever, and my heads get all clogged up—boy, is it depressing.

➥ *Kitsuke* refers to the way a kimono is put on. It takes skill and experience to adjust the obi, cords, and folds so that a kimono fits well. In the past, most Japanese women could do it themselves, but that skill has been lost as dresses, skirts, blouses, and slacks have become the common wear for day-to-day life. These days, if a woman wants to wear a kimono to, say, a wedding ceremony, she probably goes to a beauty parlor to be dressed by a professional fitter.

ぶすっと (busutto)   N / B

(1) The sound or feeling of a thick, soft material being pierced by a sharp, hard object (N). (2) Used to describe sullen anger or discontent (B).

❑ 氷を割っていて、アイスピックでぶすっと指を刺しちゃったのよ。痛かったわ。

Kōri o watte ite, aisupikku de busutto yubi o sashichatta no yo. Itakatta wa.

When I was breaking the ice, I jabbed my finger with the ice pick. It really hurt.

❑ あのお店の人はいつもぶすっとしていて愛想*がないわね。

Ano omise no hito wa itsumo busutto shite ite aiso ga nai wa ne.

The clerks at that store aren't very friendly. They always seem to be sulking.

* *Aiso*: amiability, sociability, hospitality.

めそめそ (mesomeso)   B

Whimpering, whining, sniveling. Often used to describe a timorous person who breaks into tears over trifles.

❑ 失恋*ぐらいでいつまでもめそめそするなよ。

Shitsuren gurai de itsu made mo mesomeso suru na yo.

Just because you have a broken heart, don't keep moaning and groaning about it forever.

* *Shitsuren*: disappointed or unrequited love.

❑ めそめそ泣いてばかりいないで、たまには気分転換*でもしたらどうだ。

Mesomeso naite bakari inai de, tama ni wa kibun-tenkan de mo shitara dō da.

Don't just sit around whimpering like a baby! Do something different for a change.

* *Kibun-tenkan*: a change of mood.

ぎゃあぎゃあ (gyāgyā)   B

(1) The sound of noisy crying or screeching by children, birds, animals, etc. With animals, the word can imply an unpleasant or eerie feeling. (2) Complaining, bitching, whining, griping.

❑ 隣の赤ん坊がぎゃあぎゃあ夜泣きするんで、このところ寝不足だよ。

Tonari no akanbō ga gyāgyā yonaki suru n' de, kono tokoro nebusoku da yo.

The baby next door has been bawling at night, so I haven't gotten much sleep lately.

❏ 女房子供にぎゃあぎゃあせがまれて、連休にディズニーランドへ行ってきたんだ。

Nyōbō kodomo ni gyāgyā segamarete, renkyū ni Dizunīrando e itte kita n' da.

My wife and kids had been pestering me about it, so we went to Disneyland over the long weekend.

A Spat

TARO

Mr. and Mrs. Ogawa are in their eighth year of marriage. They expected to have a good time playing tennis on Sunday afternoon, but...

72

A Spat

由美　「昼間のあなたは何よ。恥ずかしいったらありゃしない＊。女の子に**じいっと**見とれちゃって。」

厚　　「何を**ぷりぷり**してるのかと思ったらそんなことか。」

由美　「そんなことじゃありませんよ。みっともない。」

厚　　「**ぴちぴち**した若い子に見とれてどこが悪いんだよ。」

由美　「思い出しても**ぞうっと**するわ。**にたにた**鼻の下を伸ばしちゃって†さ。」

厚　　「おまえだってあやしいもんだよ。コーチと**いちゃいちゃ**してたじゃないか。」

由美　「そんなんじゃないわよ、失礼ね。あなたこそ何よ。ギャルが隣に来ただけで**そわそわ**しちゃって。いい年してばかみたい。」

厚　　「ばかみたいで悪かった❖な。」

由美　「だいたい今時若い女の子に**ちやほや**してもらおうなんて甘いわ。その**ぷよぷよ**のお腹。どこから見たって単なるおじさんのくせに✿。」

厚　　「その単なるおじさんに**めろめろ**だったのはどこのどいつ✚だよ。」

＊ *Arya shinai*: emphatic negative (contraction of *ari wa shinai*) following *tara*.

† *Hana no shita o nobasu*: lit., "to stretch out the underside of the nose," i.e., the supposedly lascivious upper lip.

❖ *Warukatta*: roughly, "that was a disservice"; I'm sorry; excuse me (used here sarcastically).

✿ *Kuse ni*: in spite of the fact that (used derogatorily).

✚ *Doitsu*: who (derogatorily).

Yumi: *Hiruma no anata wa nani yo. Hazukashii ttara arya shinai. Onna no ko ni jūtto mitorechatte.*

Atsushi: *Nani o puripuri shite 'ru no ka to omottara sonna koto ka.*

Yumi: *Sonna koto ja arimasen yo. Mittomo-nai.*

Atsushi: *Pichipichi shita wakai ko ni mitorete doko ga warui n' da yo.*

Yumi: *Omoidashite mo zōtto suru wa. Nitanita hana no shita o nobashichatte sa.*

Atsushi: *Omae datte ayashii mon da yo. Kōchi to ichaicha shite 'ta ja nai ka.*

Yumi: *Sonna n' koto ja nai wa yo, shitsurei ne. Anata koso nani yo. Gyaru ga tonari ni kita dake de sowasowa shichatte. Ii toshi shite baka mitai.*

Atsushi: *Baka mitai de warukatta na.*

Yumi: *Daitai ima-doki wakai onna no ko ni chiyahoya shite moraō nante amai wa yo. Sono buyobuyo no onaka. Doko kara mita tte tan-naru ojisan no kuse ni.*

Atsushi: *Sonna tan-naru ojisan ni meromero datta no wa doko no doitsu da yo.*

☆

Yumi: What got into you this afternoon? I was so embarrassed I could have died. Ogling all the girls in sight…

Atsushi: I wondered what you've been pissed off about. So that's all it was.

Yumi: Don't give me any "So that's all it was." You were simply disgusting.

Atsushi: What's so bad about admiring some bright-eyed young women?

Yumi: It gives me the creeps just thinking about it. Smirking away and your tongue hanging out…

Atsushi: What about you? (You looked sort of fishy yourself.) You and the instructor were hitting it off pretty well.

Yumi: That shows how much you know. The nerve! You're the one who got all flustered as soon as some young girl came by. And at your age! Boy, did you look stupid.

Atsushi: Well, excuse *me*.

Yumi: Really, you're fooling yourself if you think that young girls are going to make a fuss over you at your age. Look at that paunch! Whichever way you look at it, you're nothing but another guy who's over the hill.

Atsushi: And who was it who fell head-over-heels for that over-the-hill guy?

じいっと／じっと (jītto/jitto) N

To stay fixed or motionless, especially when staring at something or when enduring something painful or difficult. While *jitto* emphasizes the condition of motionless concentration, *jītto* stresses the duration.

❏ そんなにじいっと見つめないで。

Sonna ni jītto mitsumenai de.

Stop staring at me like that.

❏ 子供はちっともじっとしていないから、休む間もないんです。

Kodomo wa chittomo jitto shite inai kara, yasumu ma mo nai n' desu.

My kids can't keep still, so I never have a moment's peace.

ぷりぷり (puripuri) B

To get angry, to be in a bad mood.

❏ ワイシャツに口紅がついていたって、女房はぷりぷり怒っているんですよ。

Waishatsu ni kuchibeni ga tsuite ita tte, nyōbō wa puripuri okotte iru n' desu yo.

My wife says there was lipstick on my shirt, and now she's hopping mad.

❏ 課長は朝からぷりぷりして物も言わないけど、一体*何があったんですか。

Kachō wa asa kara puripuri shite mono mo iwanai kedo, ittai nani ga atta n' desu ka.

The section chief has been grumpy and not saying much since morning. What on earth happened?

* *Ittai*: lit., "in one body, all in all"; here colloquial "ever, on earth" expressing strong doubt.

ぴちぴち (pichipichi) G / N

(1) The sound or feeling of a small object bouncing or flapping in a lively manner. Often used to describe live fish. (2) By extension, a spirited, active person—usually a young woman who is full of vim and vigor.

❑ 魚はやっぱりぴちぴちと生きがいいのじゃないとおいしくないよね。

Sakana wa yappari pichipichi to iki ga ii no ja nai to oishiku nai yo ne.

You know, fish just doesn't taste good unless it's nice and fresh.

❑ 新入社員は、ぴちぴちしてまぶしいくらいだよ。

Shinnyū-shain wa, pichipichi shite mabushii kurai da yo.

Those new girls we've hired are so fresh-faced and bright-eyed that you're almost blinded by the dazzle.

ぞうっと／ぞっと (zōtto/zotto) B

To shiver with sudden cold or fright so that one's hair seems to stand on end. *Zōtto* is the more emphatic.

❑ 突然ぞうっと寒気が襲ってきたので熱を計ってみたら、9度もあったんです。

Totsuzen zōtto samuke ga osotte kita no de netsu o hakatte mitara, ku-do mo atta n' desu.

All of a sudden I came down with the chills, and when I took my temperature, it said 39°C (102.2°F).

❑ 高所恐怖症だから、高層ビルの窓から下をのぞき込んだりするとぞっとするの。

Kōsho–kyōfu-shō da kara, kōsō-biru no mado kara shita o nozokikondari suru to zotto suru no.

I have acrophobia, so I get the jitters when I do anything like look down from the window of a skyscraper.

にたにた (nitanita) B

To smirk, to display a sinister smile or grin. Used to describe a person who seems to be hiding some secret, unseemly pleasure or scheme.

❑ にたにたしていないで、はっきり言ったらどうなの。

Nitanita shite inai de, hakkiri ittara dō na no.

Stop smirking and say what's on your mind (come out with it).

❑ 君、社長に向かってそのにたにた笑いは何だね、失礼だよ。

Kimi, shachō ni mukatte sono nitanita-warai wa nan da ne, shitsurei da yo.

Hey there. What do you think you're doing, smirking at the company president like that? It's downright rude.

いちゃいちゃ (ichaicha) B

Used to describe a couple engaging in a public display of affection, particularly when viewed as unsavory by others.

❏ 会社の中でいちゃいちゃしてるなんて、言語道断*だよ。

Kaisha no naka de ichaicha shite 'ru nante, gongo-dōdan da yo.

It's simply outrageous the way those two make like little lovebirds right in the office.

 * *Gongo-dōdan*: lit., "the way is closed to language"; unspeakably bad.

❏ パッケージ・ツアーも考えものだね。新婚さんにいちゃいちゃあてつけられて*まいったよ。

Pakkēji-tsuā mo kangaemono da ne. Shinkon-san ni ichaicha atetsuke-rarete maitta yo.

You should think twice about going on a package tour. I got stuck with a bunch of spooning newlyweds.

 * *Atetsukeru*: to annoy or do something out of spite; to parade or flaunt affectionate relations.

➡ Japanese tradition has long frowned on men and women holding hands, kissing, or showing affection in public. This is due in part to the influence of Confucianism, which held that boys and girls should be kept apart after the age of seven. Visit a park in Japan on a Sunday afternoon, though, and you will see that the younger generation is not taking this old moral code too seriously.

そわそわ (sowasowa) N / B

To be distracted, nervous, unable to settle down.

❏ さっきから時計ばかり気にして、そわそわしているけど、何か約束でもあるの。

Sakki kara tokei bakari ki ni shite, sowasowa shite 'ru kedo, nani ka yaku-soku de mo aru no.

You keep looking at your watch and fidgeting. Do you have an appointment or something?

❏ どうもそわそわと落ち着かないと思ったら、高木さん、今日お見合いなんですって。

Dōmo sowasowa to ochitsukanai to omottara, Takagi-san, kyō omiai nan desu tte.

Mr. Takagi seemed to be on pins and needles. It turns out that he has an *omiai* today.

➡ Many Japanese still get married by means of arranged introductions called 見合い *miai* (or *omiai*). Men and women who are interested in meeting potential marriage partners give their résumés, called 釣り書き *tsurigaki*, together with photographs, to an acquaintance who has agreed to arrange the meeting. This person then finds couples with compatible family and educational backgrounds, occupations, assets, physical attributes, etc., exchanges the *tsurigaki* and photo, and suggests a meeting. Either party is free to decline at this stage. If both are interested, a time and place are set up for them to be introduced. (A good place to snoop on *omiai* in progress is the coffee shop of a luxury hotel on a weekend afternoon.) After the meeting, the couple usually go on a few dates by themselves, after which time they decide whether or not to continue meeting with the ultimate goal being marriage.

The phrase 見合い結婚 *miai kekkon* is often translated as "arranged marriage." This is misleading, though, since it suggests that the marriage is arranged by the family without the consent of the parties involved. While such marriages were once common in Japan, especially among the upper classes, nearly all people who take part in *omiai* today do so voluntarily. In recent years, 恋愛結婚 *ren'ai kekkon*—often translated as "love marriage"—has become by far the more common practice.

ちやほや (chiyahoya) B
To fuss over, spoil, butter up. Generally in a critical sense.

❑ おばあちゃん子でちやほやと育てられたから、彼はわがままなところがあるんだよ。

Obāchan-ko de chiyahoya to sodaterareta kara, kare wa wagamama na tokoro ga aru n' da yo.

He was spoiled by his grandmother (he was a grandma's little boy) when he was growing up, so now he's a bit selfish.

❑ 社長の娘だからとまわりがちやほやするから、ますます本人も増長* するんだよ。

Shachō no musume da kara to mawari ga chiyahoya suru kara, masu-masu honnin mo zōchō suru n' da yo.

Since she's the president's daughter and everyone makes a big fuss over her, she's getting more and more stuck up.

* *Zōchō*: to grow gradually worse; to become increasingly arrogant.

ぷよぷよ (buyobuyo) B

Squishy, squelchy, flabby, puffy, bloated. Used to describe a soft, liquid-filled object, especially one that is unpleasant to the touch or sight.

❑ 天ぷらを揚げてたら油がはねて、手にぷよぷよの水ぶくれができちゃったのよ。痛いわ。

Tempura o agete 'tara abura ga hanete, te ni buyobuyo no mizubukure ga dekichatta no yo. Itai wa.

I got spattered with oil when I was cooking tempura, and now I have a big, squishy blister on my hand. My, does it hurt.

❑ いくら温泉が気持ちいいからといっても、そんなに入ってたらふやけて*ぷよぷよになるぞ。

Ikura onsen ga kimochi ii kara to itte mo, sonna ni haitte 'tara fuyakete buyobuyo ni naru zo.

I know it feels good to be soaking yourself in the hot spring, but you're going to get water-logged if you stay in too long.

* *Fuyakeru*: to swell up, get soggy.

めろめろ (meromero) N / B

Limp, floppy, spineless, unable to stand up straight. Often used to criticize someone's weakness or lack of resolve.

❑ あの会社はワンマン社長が倒れて、今めろめろになっているみたいだよ。

Ano kaisha wa wanman-shachō ga taorete, ima meromero ni natte iru mitai da yo.

Ever since its all-powerful president fell ill, that company has sort of come apart at the seams.

❑ 恵子は今彼にめろめろだから、何を言っても耳に入らないわよ。

Keiko wa ima kare ni meromero da kara, nani o itte mo mimi ni hairanai wa yo.

Right now Keiko is all moony (has gone cuckoo) over him. No matter what you say to her, it goes in one ear and out the other.

Smoothing Things Over

Mr. and Mrs. Hasegawa are approaching their mid-thirties. Before going to sleep one Sunday night, they have a talk in the bedroom.

Smoothing Things Over

京子 「ねえ、あなた、この頃**つるつる**になってきたような気がしない？」

隆 「なっ、何だよ急に。」（と、近頃薄くなってきた頭に思わず手をやる）

京子 「**てかてか**っていうほどでもないけどさ。」

隆 「冗談じゃないよ。それはない*よ。」

京子 「そうかしら。お手当ては早め早めが肝心なのよね。最近いいのが出てるのよ。ちょっと高いけど。お隣も使っていらっしゃるんですって。」

隆 「ふうん。」

京子 「朝と晩、**せっせ**と付けて**ぴしゃぴしゃ**たたくようにするといいんですって。」

隆 「どのくらいで効くのかなあ。」

京子 「そりゃあ、**めきめき**というわけにはいかないでしょうけど。**じわじわ**効いてくるんじゃない？」

隆 「高いっていくら？」

京子 「うふふ。実はね、もう買っちゃったんだ。お客様のお肌に**ぴったり**ですって勧められたんだもん。」

隆 「何だよそれ。」

京子 「あら、美顔クリームに決まってるじゃない。**しっとりつやつや**になったでしょう。」

隆 「おいおい、いくらだよ。」

京子 「２万円。**すべすべ**のお肌が買えると思えば安いものよね、あなた。」

---

* *Sore wa nai*: more empathic version of *sonna koto wa nai* ("it's nothing like that," "no way!").

Kyōko: *Nē, anata, konogoro tsurutsuru ni natte kita yō na ki ga shinai?*

Takashi: *Na—, nan da yo kyū ni. (to, chikagoro usuku natte kita atama ni omowazu te o yaru)*

Kyōko: *Tekateka tte iu hodo de mo nai kedo sa.*

Takashi: *Jōdan ja nai yo. Sore wa nai yo.*

Kyōko: *Sō kashira. Oteate wa hayame-hayame ga kanjin na no yo ne. Saikin ii no ga dete 'ru no yo. Chotto takai kedo. Otonari mo tsukatte irassharu n' desu tte.*

Takashi: *Fūn.*

Kyōko: *Asa to ban, sesseto tsukete pishapisha tataku yō ni suru to ii n' desu tte.*

Takashi: *Dono kurai de kiku no ka nā.*

Kyōko: *Soryā, mekimeki to iu wake ni wa ikanai deshō kedo. Jiwajiwa kiite kuru n' ja nai?*

Takashi: *Takai tte ikura?*

Kyōko: *Ufufu. Jitsu wa ne, mō katchatta n' da. Okyaku-sama no ohada ni pittari desu tte susumerareta n' da mon.*

Takashi: *Nan da yo sore.*

Kyōko: *Ara, bigan-kurīmu ni kimatte 'ru ja nai. Shittori tsuyatsuya ni natta deshō.*

Takashi: *Oioi, ikura da yo.*

Kyōko: *Ni-man'en. Subesube no ohada ga kaeru to omoeba yasui mono yo ne, anata.*

☆

Kyōko: Say, honey. Haven't you noticed how much smoother it's become these days, sort of like a billiard ball?

Takashi: Wha—, what brings that on? (Without thinking, he touches his recently thinning hair.)

Kyōko: I wouldn't go so far as to call it slick, though.

Takashi: You've got to be kidding! It's not that bad!

Kyōko: You think so? It's awfully important to start treatment as soon as possible. Some good stuff has come out lately. It's a little expensive, but I hear our next-door neighbor is using it.

Takashi: Hmm.

Kyōko: They say it works if you keep steadily at it every morning and night, practically slapping it on.

Takashi: I wonder how long it takes to work.

Kyōko: It's not by leaps and bounds, I imagine. It probably more like slow and steady.

Takashi: How expensive is "expensive"?

Kyōko: Hee-hee. As a matter of fact, I've already bought some. They *recommended* it to me. Said it would be perfect for my skin.

Takashi: Bought some! What did you buy?

Kyōko: Why, facial cream, of course. Doesn't my skin look so much moister and glowing?

Takashi: For crying out loud! How much did it cost?

Kyōko: Twenty thousand yen. Don't you think that's a bargain for nice, smooth skin, honey?

つるつる (tsurutsuru) G / N / B

(1) Smooth, shiny, slick (G/N/B). (2) To slide smoothly across a flat surface (N). (3) The sound or feeling of slurping or ingesting something that has a smooth surface. Often used to describe the eating of soba, udon, or other noodle-like food (N).

❑ お肌がつるつるになるっていうからこのクリームを買ったのに、かぶれちゃったわ。

Ohada ga tsurutsuru ni naru tte iu kara kono kurīmu o katta no ni, kaburechatta wa.

I bought this cream because they said it would make my skin nice and smooth. Instead I broke out in a rash.

❑ きのうの雪が凍って道路がつるつるだから、足元に気をつけてね。

Kinō no yuki ga kōtte dōro ga tsurutsuru da kara, ashimoto ni ki o tsukete ne.

Yesterday's snow has turned to ice. The streets are slippery, so watch your step.

❏ 夏は冷や麦をつるつるやるっていうのが最高だね。

Natsu wa hiyamugi o tsurutsuru yaru tte iu no ga saikō da ne.

In summer there's nothing like slurping down some nice cool *hiyamugi* (thin *udon* served with water and ice).

➡ Japan is a noodle mecca. Even the smallest towns have shops selling ラーメン *rāmen* (Chinese noodles served in a hot broth), and the fried chow mein called 焼きそば *yakisoba* is often sold from stalls at neighborhood festivals and other public events. Italian spaghetti is popular as well. Besides these recent imports, Japan has two main types of indigenous noodles: そば *soba* and うどん *udon*.

Soba is made from buckwheat flour combined with plain wheat flour, yams, egg whites, and other ingredients. The batter is mixed with water and rolled into a flat crust, which is then sliced into thin strips to form the noodles. It can be eaten with each mouthful dipped into a broth flavored with soy sauce, or it may be served in hot broth in a wide-brimmed bowl. Soba is particularly popular in the Kantō region.

Udon is prepared in the same way as *soba*, but instead of buckwheat flour the raw material is plain wheat flour. Its origins in Japan are said to date back to the Nara Period (701–784), when wonton was introduced from China. *Udon* noodles are fatter and whiter than *soba*, but they are eaten in much the same way. In Kansai, *udon* is more popular than *soba*.

Two particularly tasty versions of udon that are popular during the hot summer months are 冷や麦 *hiyamugi* and そうめん *sōmen*. Usually sold in dry form like spaghetti, the noodles are boiled in water and then cooled with ice or cold water. Then they are dipped into a soy-sauce-flavored broth and eaten. *Hiyamugi* noodles are a bit fatter than *sōmen*, and they are often eaten from a bowl of cold water.

Proper Japanese manners call for a healthy slurping noise when eating noodles. Noodles served in a hot broth become gooey and lose their flavor if they're left standing, so people generally like to eat them while they are still piping hot. To avoid burning the mouth, Japanese have developed the habit of inhaling air with the noodles. This cools off the food and lets you savor the broth at the same time. If you eat noodles without accompanying noises, people will think you don't like the taste. (Basically, this rule applies only to noodles. With other kinds of food, loud munching or smacking noises are frowned upon.)

てかてか (tekateka) N / B

The shiny appearance of a smooth surface. Often in reference to something cheap-looking.

❏ 制服のズボンのお尻がすりきれててかてかになっちゃった。

Seifuku no zubon no oshiri ga surikirete tekateka ni natchatta.

The seat of my uniform pants has worn so thin it's started to shine.

❏ ポマードでてかてかの頭なんて、今時はやらないわよね。

Pomādo de tekateka no atama nante, ima-doki hayaranai wa yo ne.

In this day and age *nobody* slicks down his hair with hair oil (pomade) anymore.

せっせと (sesseto) G / N

With steady and uninterrupted diligence.

❏ せっせと貯金をしても、こう金利が低くてはねえ。

Sesseto chōkin o shite mo, kō kinri ga hikukute wa nē.

I put money in the bank as regular as clockwork, but with the interest rates so low, you know…

❏ せっせと立ち働いているお母さんの姿を見たら、涙が出たわ。

Sesseto tachihataraite iru okāsan no sugata o mitara, namida ga deta wa.

Seeing my mother working as busy as a bee, I couldn't keep the tears from my eyes.

ぴしゃぴしゃ (pishapisha) N

The sound or feeling of something soft (like drops of water) and often flat (such as the palm of the hand) hitting against a soft or wet surface.

❏ 子供のお尻をぴしゃぴしゃたたいてお仕置きするような親なんて、近頃いなくなったね。

Kodomo no oshiri o pishapisha tataite oshioki suru yō na oya nante, chikagoro inaku natta ne.

There aren't any parents around these days who discipline their children by giving their little behinds a good spanking.

❏ 雨の日はぴしゃぴしゃはねをあげちゃう*から、外に出るのがおっくうなのよね。

Ame no hi wa pishapisha hane o agechau kara, soto ni deru no ga okkū na no yo ne.

I really hate going out on rainy days because my legs get all spattered with water.

> * *Hane o ageru*: lit., "to raise jumps"; i.e., to create splashes, to splash, to spatter (oneself or one's own clothing).

めきめき (mekimeki) G

Used to describe quick progress, growth, recovery, etc.

❑ 書道を始めたとは聞いてたけど、あんまりめきめき腕が上がった*
んで驚いたよ。

*Shodō o hajimeta to wa kiite 'ta kedo, anmari mekimeki ude ga agatta n'
de odoroita yo.*

I heard she'd started doing calligraphy, but I was really surprised by how
fast she'd gotten the hang of it.

* *Ude ga agaru*: to have one's skills improve in a practical skill or art.

❑ 小学校の時には背が低い方だったんだけど、中学に入ってからめき
めき伸びたんだ。

*Shōgakkō no toki ni wa se ga hikui hō datta n' da kedo, chūgaku ni haitte
kara mekimeki nobita n' da.*

I was short all through elementary school, but after getting into junior
high I shot up like a beanstalk.

じわじわ (jiwajiwa) N

Growing or progressing slowly but steadily.

❑ 冬なのに、今日は日中じわじわと汗ばむような陽気だったね。

Fuyu na no ni, kyō wa nitchū jiwajiwa to asebamu yō na yōki datta ne.

Although it's winter, the weather today was so fine during the daytime
that you actually started to work up a sweat.

❑ 漢方薬は即効性はないけど、じわじわきいてきて副作用が少ないん
ですって。

*Kanpō-yaku wa sokkō-sei wa nai kedo, jiwajiwa kiite kite fuku-sayō ga
sukunai n' desu tte.*

They say Chinese herbal medicine isn't quick to take effect, but it works
little by little and doesn't have many side effects.

ぴったり／ぴたり (pittari/pitari) G / N

(1) Perfectly matched, on target, just right, completely suitable
(G/N). (2) Solidly attached, tightly closed (N). (3) Used to describe a
continuous action that comes to a complete or sudden stop (N). The
meanings of *pittari* and *pitari* are very similar, with *pittari* used for
emphasis and *pitari* when the meaning is "on target." The choice for
"completely suitable" is usually *pittari*. When the word is used as an
adjectival verb followed by *da* or *na*, only the *pittari* form is
possible.

❑ この背広、まるであつらえたように君にぴったりだね。

Kono sebiro, maru de atsuraeta yō ni kimi ni pittari da ne.

That suit fits you so well it looks like it was tailor-made.

❏ あの占い師は何でもぴたりと当てちゃうんですって。

Ano uranai-shi wa nan de mo pitari to atechau n' desu tte.

They say that fortune-teller hits the nail on the head about everything (every time).

❏ 車にはったステッカーが、ぴったりとくっついて離れないの。困るわ。

Kuruma ni hatta sutekkā ga, pittari to kuttsuite hanarenai no. Komaru wa.

The sticker on my car is stuck on so hard that it just won't come off. Darn!

❏ 横山さん、医者に注意されてから、タバコをぴたりとやめたらしいよ。

Yokoyama-san, isha ni chūi sarete kara, tabako o pitari to yameta rashii yo.

Apparently Mr. Yokoyama quit smoking cold turkey as soon as he was warned by his doctor.

しっとり (shittori) G

(1) Moist. Often used to describe skin that is soft to the touch. (2) Calm, quiet, relaxed, soothing. Can be used to describe people, the atmosphere of a place, etc. When describing a woman, *shittori* suggests that she is graceful, calm, gentle.

❏ 私は乾燥肌だから、久美子さんみたいなしっとりした潤いのある肌にあこがれるわ。

Watashi wa kansō-hada da kara, Kumiko-san mitai na shittori shita uruoi no aru hada ni akogareru wa.

My skin is the dry type, so I really envy moist, smooth skin like yours, Kumiko.

❏ たまには仕事を離れて温泉にでもつかって、しっとりとした気分を味わいたいものだね。

Tama ni wa shigoto o hanarete onsen ni de mo tsukatte, shittori to shita kibun o ajiwaitai mono da ne.

Sometimes I want to get away from work, soak in some hot springs, and enjoy a mood of complete tranquillity.

❏ 康子さんは、着物の似合うしっとりとした雰囲気の人だね。

Yasuko-san wa, kimono no niau shittori to shita fun'iki no hito da ne.

Yasuko has an air of gentle grace, so a kimono looks good on her.

つやつや (tsuyatsuya) G

Shining, glistening, sparkling. Often used to describe skin, hair, feathers, leather, etc.

❑ つやつやした黒い髪のことを、からすのぬれ羽色っていうのよ。

Tsuyatsuya shita kuroi kami no koto o, karasu no nureba-iro tte iu no yo.

The phrase "the color of wet raven feathers" is used to describe beautifully shiny black hair.

❑ いつもつやつやの肌をしていらっしゃるけれど、何かお手入れの秘けつがあるんですか。

Itsumo tsuyatsuya no hada o shite irassharu keredo, nani ka oteire no hiketsu ga aru n' desu ka.

Your skin is always glowing. Do you have some secret method of skin care?

すべすべ (subesube) G

Smooth and pleasing to the touch.

❑ ハンドクリームをぬって寝れば、水仕事で荒れた手もすべすべになりますよ。

Hando-kurīmu o nutte nereba, mizu-shigoto de areta te mo subesube ni narimasu yo.

If you put on some hand cream before you go to sleep, your dishpan hands will become nice and smooth.

❑ 柔らかくてすべすべで、まるで赤ちゃんのような肌ですね。

Yawarakakute subesube de, maru de akachan no yō na hada desu ne.

Your skin is so white and soft and delicate, just like a baby's.

❑ この建物、ずいぶん古いんでしょうね。階段の手すりもすべすべになっていますからね。

Kono tatemono, zuibun furui n' deshō ne. Kaidan no tesuri mo subesube ni natte imasu kara ne.

This building must be very old. Even the banisters have been worn smooth.

"Pretty Woman"

Two female office workers, Yoshiko Sugiyama and Kaori Yasuda, are in a coffee shop talking about movies.

"Pretty Woman"

良子 「『プリティ・ウーマン』を見たんですって？ どうだった？」

香織 「すっごくよかったわよ。おすすめだわ。」

良子 「どんなところが？」

香織 「**はらはらどきどき**の連続なのよ。それに何といってもリチャード・ギアがカッコイイの！」

良子 「彼氏*といったんでしょ。」

香織 「まあね。とにかく、ジュリア・ロバーツもかわいいし。もう**ぼうっとしちゃった**†わよ。」

良子 「ふうん。」

香織 「最初は**ぱっと**しない彼女がさあ、見違えるようにきれいになっちゃうのよね。」

良子 「やっぱり女は男次第ってことなのかしら。」

香織 「ラストがまたいいのよ。オープン・カーでバラの花を持って彼女を迎えにいくんだけどさ。リチャード・ギアには**うっとり**よね。」

良子 「いいなあ、香織は。**しっかり**した彼もいるしさ。」

香織 「あれはやめたわ。**はっきり**言ってもう**うんざり**。」

良子 「なぜ？」

香織 「映画の後、何を食べたと思う？ 焼き肉定食†よ。**がばがば**ビールは飲むし。もう最低。**がっくり**よ。」

---

* *Kareshi*: boyfriend.

† *Yakiniku-teishoku*: see note following English translation.

Yoshiko: *"Puritī-ūman" o mita n' desu tte? Dō datta?*

Kaori: *Sugoku yokatta wa yo. Osusume da wa.*

Yoshiko: *Donna tokoro ga?*

Kaori: *Harahara dokidoki no renzoku na no yo. Sore ni nan to itte mo Richādo Gia ga kakko ii no!*

Yoshiko: *Kareshi to itta n' desho.*

Kaori: *Mā ne. Tonikaku, Juria Robātsu mo kawaii shi. Mō pōtto shichatta wa yo.*

Yoshiko: *Fūn.*

Kaori: *Saisho wa patto shinai kanojo ga sā, michigaeru yō ni kirei ni natchau no yo ne.*

Yoshiko: *Yappari onna wa otoko-shidai tte koto na no kashira.*

Kaori: *Rasuto ga mata ii no yo. Ōpun-kā de bara no hana o motte kanojo o mukae ni iku n' da kedo sa. Richādo Gia ni wa uttori yo ne.*

Yoshiko: *Ii nā, Kaori wa. Shikkari shita kare mo iru shi sa.*

Kaori: *Are wa yameta wa. Hakkiri itte mō unzari.*

Yoshiko: *Naze?*

Kaori: *Eiga no ato, nani o tabeta to omou? Yakiniku-teishoku yo. Gabagaba bīru wa nomu shi. Mō saitei. Gakkuri yo.*

☆

Yoshiko: So you saw "Pretty Woman"? How was it?

Kaori: Absolutely fantastic. I highly recommend it.

Yoshiko: What was so good about it?

Kaori: It keeps you on the edge of your seat from beginning to end. And best of all, Richard Gere is just so cool!

Yoshiko: You went with your boyfriend, right?

Kaori: Yeah, well… Anyhow, Julia Roberts is cute, too. I was practically in a daze.

Yoshiko: Hmm.

Kaori: At first she's not much to speak of, but later on she's so beautiful you'd hardly recognize her.

Yoshiko: So maybe it's true that a woman is only as good as her man.

Kaori: The last scene was good, too. He comes in this convertible with some roses to pick her up. Richard Gere really knocks me out.

Yoshiko: How neat for you, Kaori. And you've got such a reliable boyfriend, too.

Kaori: No, I dumped him. To tell you the truth, I just got fed up.

Yoshiko: How come?

Kaori: After the movie, guess what we had to eat? *Yakiniku-teishoku*, that's what. And he was guzzling beer on top of that. What a bummer!

➥ The most popular restaurants for a young man to take his girlfriend in Japan are French or Italian, for European cuisine has a stylish, sophisticated image. She's likely to be disappointed if he chooses instead ラーメン *rāmen* "Chinese noodles," ギョーザ *gyōza* "meat dumplings," or 焼き肉定食 *yakiniku-teishoku* "barbecued beef set"; in other words, inexpensive food, served in inelegant surroundings.

A *yakiniku-teishoku* consists of thinly sliced Korean-style barbecued beef accompanied by rice, soup, and perhaps some onions or vegetables. Popular with office workers on lunch break, *teishoku* sets can be prepared and eaten quickly and are cheaper than à la carte. Other common *teishoku* are 焼き魚定食 *yakizakana-teishoku* "fried fish set" and とんかつ定食 *tonkatsu-teishoku* "pork cutlet set."

はらはら (harahara) N / B

(1) To worry or fret about how things will turn out. Primarily used to describe a passive observer's anxiety at watching something that is dangerous or frightening (N/B). (2) The feeling or appearance of small, light objects—flower petals, leaves, rain, dewdrops, tears—falling gently a few at a time. In this sense, *harahara* often suggests a melancholy feeling about the passage of time (N).

❏ 君の運転にははらはらさせられるよ。ちっともバックミラーを見ていないんだもの。

Kimi no unten ni wa harahara saserareru yo. Chittomo bakku-mirā o mite inai n' da mono.

Your driving scares me to death. You never even glance at the rearview mirror.

❑ はらはらと桜の花が散るのを見ていると、この世の無常を感じるね。

Harahara to sakura no hana ga chiru no o mite iru to, kono yo no mujō o kanjiru ne.

Watching the cherry blossoms flutter down makes you realize how fleeting life is.

どきどき (dokidoki) G / N / B

The sound or feeling of rapid, pounding heartbeats caused by worry, fear, surprise, sudden exercise, or excited expectation. While *harahara* expresses one's nervousness about some event occurring outside oneself, *dokidoki* refers to one's reaction to something one is directly involved in.

❑ 駅の階段を駆け上がっただけでどきどきするなんて、我ながら情けないよ。

Eki no kaidan o kakeagatta dake de dokidoki suru nante, ware-nagara nasake-nai yo.

It's pretty sad, even if I do say so myself, the way my heart starts pounding when I just run up the stairs at the train station.

❑ 君に振られるんじゃないかと思って、内心どきどきしていたんだ。

Kimi ni furareru n' ja nai ka to omotte, naishin dokidoki shite ita n' da.

I was beside myself with worry, thinking you were going to jilt me.

ぽうっと (pōtto) G / N

(1) To be so distracted or obsessed with something that you don't notice what is happening right in front of you (N). (2) A bright, reddish appearance (G/N). In either sense, *pōtto* often suggests the feeling of blood rushing to one's head.

❑ 田村さん、ぽうっとしていると思ったら、新入社員の村上さんに一目ぼれしたらしいのよ。

Tamura-san, pōtto shite iru to omottara, shinyū-shain no Murakami-san ni hitome-bore shita rashii no yo.

I had the feeling Miss Tamura was going around in a daze. Apparently she fell for the new employee Mr. Murakami at first sight.

❑ 私、お酒は弱いんです。すぐぽうっと顔が赤くなっちゃって。

Watashi, osake wa yowai n' desu. Sugu pōtto kao ga akaku natchatte.

I'm not a very good drinker. My face immediately turns as red as a beet.

ぱっと／ぱあっと (patto/pātto) G / N

(1) Showy, gaudy, spectacular. In this meaning, *patto* is usually used

in the negative form, *patto shinai,* meaning dull, somber, unsatisfactory. However, the version with the long vowel, *pātto,* does not have the negative form (G/N). (2) A quick or sudden motion or change (N). (3) A spreading or widening action (N).

☑ 営業成績は今ひとつ*ぱっとしないが、今夜はぱあっと派手に繰り出そう†、諸君。

Eigyō-seiseki wa ima-hitotsu patto shinai ga, kon'ya wa pātto hade ni kuridasō, shokun.

Our sales aren't much to brag about, boys, but let's go out tonight and paint the town red anyway.

* *Ima-hitotsu:* not quite enough, lacking.
† *Kuridasu:* to flock, turn out in force.

❑ 子供は道路でもぱっと飛び出すから危ないわね。

Kodomo wa dōro de mo patto tobidasu kara abunai wa ne.

It's dangerous how children dash out into the street.

❑ 人の噂はぱっと広まるから怖いよ。

Hito no uwasa wa patto hiromaru kara kowai yo.

It's frightening how fast gossip spreads.

うっとり (uttori) G

To be enraptured by the beauty of something.

❑ 玉三郎*の舞台はやっぱりいいわね。あまりの美しさにうっとり見とれちゃったわ。

Tamasaburō no butai wa yappari ii wa ne. Amari no utsukushisa ni uttori mitorechatta wa.

Tamasaburō's performances really are great. I was overwhelmed by the sheer beauty of it.

* *Tamasaburō:* Bandō (坂東) Tamasaburō, Kabuki actor specializing in female roles, born 1950; the fifth in a line of actors using this name since the early nineteenth century.

❑ 育子さんはピアノがすごく上手なのよ。彼女のショパンなんてうっとりと聴きほれるわ。

Ikuko-san wa piano ga sugoku jōzu na no yo. Kanojo no Shopan nante uttori to kikihoreru wa.

Ikuko is a fantastic pianist. Listening to her Chopin, I practically go into a trance.

しっかり (shikkari)　G/N/B

(1) To have a solid foundation, structure, connection, etc. (G/N). (2) Trustworthy, dependable, solid. Often used to describe a person's body, spirit, personality, intelligence, ideas, etc. Can also describe a company, source of information, or many other things (G/N). *Shikkari* sometimes refers sarcastically to a crafty or stingy person (B). (3) Referring to action and behavior: well, sufficiently, solidly, diligently (G). (4) A large number or amount (G/N).

❑ マンション選びのポイントは、まず構造がしっかりしているかどうかですよ。

Manshon-erabi no pointo wa, mazu kōzō ga shikkari shite iru ka dō ka desu yo.

The first thing you should check before buying a condominium is how solidly it's built.

❑ お父さん、しっかりしてよ。酔っぱらって玄関で寝ちゃったら風邪ひくわよ。

Otōsan, shikkari shite yo. Yopparatte genkan de nechattara kaze hiku wà yo.

Pull yourself together, Dad. You'll catch a cold if you lie down drunk like that in the entranceway.

❑ しっかりした会社に勤めていれば不況になっても安心ですね。

Shikkari shita kaisha ni tsutomete ireba fukyō ni natte mo anshin desu ne.

If you work for a solid company, you won't have to worry about a faltering economy.

❑ 女房のやつ、しっかり者でね、この5年間に100万もヘソクリしてたんだぜ。

Nyōbō no yatsu, shikkari-mono de ne, kono go-nenkan ni hyaku-man mo hesokuri shite 'ta n' da ze.

My old lady is a real tightwad. In just the past five years, man, she's stashed away all of a million yen in pin money.

❑ 学生時代にもっとしっかりと勉強しておくべきだったよ。

Gakusei-jidai ni motto shikkari to benkyō shite oku beki datta yo.

I should have studied harder when I was a student.

❑ 朝ごはんをしっかり食べるのが健康の秘けつです。

Asa gohan o shikkari taberu no ga kenkō no hiketsu desu.

The secret to good health is eating a hearty breakfast.

はっきり (hakkiri) G / N

Clear, distinct; unambiguous, unmistakable.

❑ あれからもう１５年もたつのに、まるできのうのことのようにはっきりと覚えているわ。

Are kara mō jūgo-nen mo tatsu no ni, maru de kinō no koto no yō ni hakkiri to oboete iru wa.

That was fifteen years ago, but I still remember it all as if it were yesterday.

❑ どうもはっきりしないお天気ね。

Dōmo hakkiri shinai otenki ne.

This weather sure is fickle, isn't it.

うんざり (unzari) B

To be bored, tired, fed up. To be unwilling to endure something any longer.

❑ いくら納豆が好きでも、毎朝毎晩納豆じゃうんざりするよ。

Ikura nattō ga suki de mo, maiasa maiban nattō ja unzari suru yo.

No matter how much you might like *nattō*, you'd get tired of it, too, if you ate it morning and night.

❑ お説教はもううんざりよ。自分のことは自分で決めるわ。

Osekkyō wa mō unzari yo. Jibun no koto wa jibun de kimeru wa.

I'm fed up with your sermons. I'm going to live my life the way I want to (I'll decide what's best for me).

➥ *Nattō* is made from boiled soybeans that have been fermented with a special kind of bacteria. Due to its distinctive smell and its viscous, stringy consistency, people either love it or hate it.

がばがば (gabagaba) N / B

(1) The sound or appearance of gurgling or gushing water (N/B). (2) To earn or spend a lot of money (B). (3) To be baggy, too big, in reference to clothes, hats, shoes, etc. (B).

❑ 下水ががばがばいっているんだけど、どこかつまっているのかしら。

Gesui ga gabagaba itte iru n' da kedo, doko ka tsumatte iru no kashira.

The drain pipes have been making gurgling noises. I wonder if they're clogged up somewhere.

❑ あの会社、一時は不動産でがばがばもうかっていたらしいよ。

Ano kaisha, ichiji wa fudōsan de gabagaba mōkatte ita rashii yo.

For a while, that company was apparently raking in money hand over foot from real estate.

❏ お兄ちゃんのお下がりの靴じゃ、やっぱりがばがばね。

Onīchan no osagari no kutsu ja, yappari gabagaba ne.

Big brother's hand-me-down shoes are huge on you after all, aren't they.

がっくり (gakkuri) B

(1) To bend, fall, tip over, or collapse suddenly. By extension, to become disappointed or discouraged. (2) Used to describe a sudden loss of strength, determination, or energy, especially when the change is very great.

❏ 連れ合いが亡くなって、祖父もがっくりきたらしいんだ。

Tsureai ga naku natte, sofu mo gakkuri kita rashii n' da.

Grandfather has been down in the dumps ever since his wife died.

❏ 五十の坂を越したら、がっくり体力が落ちてね、夜ふかしがまるでだめになったんだ。

Gojū no saka o koshitara, gakkuri tairyoku ga ochite ne, yofukashi ga maru de dame ni natta n' da.

After hitting fifty I don't seem to have the old oomph anymore. Staying up to all hours of the night is completely beyond me.

A Romantic Flair

Tomoko Tabuchi wants a change of mood, so she has come to the beauty parlor to have her hair done in a different style. She hopes to look more feminine, to have more of a romantic flair. The hairdresser is Seiichi Nishi.

A Romantic Flair

田淵　「秋だから、**ふわっと**ロマンチックな頭にしたいんだけど。」

西　「お客様の**おぐし***は、細くて**さらさら**なので、ストレートも悪くないと思いますけどね。」

田淵　「それがいやなのよ。雨が降ると、**ぺしゃんこ**になっちゃうし。何だか†子供っぽい感じがして。」

西　「そうですか。もったいないですね。**ごわごわ**していやだとおっしゃるお客様も多いのに。」

田淵　「そうかしら。寝癖はついて**ぼさぼさ**になるし、頭の形の悪さは**くっきり**出ちゃうし、いやだわ。」

西　「それじゃ、**ふんわり**全体にパーマをかけますか。そうすれば、**ぺたんと**なることはないでしょう。」

田淵　「でも、**ちりちり**にだけはならないようにしてよ。」

西　「おまかせください。ロマンチックに**ばっちり**決めてみせますよ。ただし、あとはお客様次第ですけどね。」

---

* *Ogushi*: hair; a polite term used largely by woman.

† *Nan da ka*: something, somehow, sort of.

Tabuchi: *Aki da kara, fuwatto romanchikku na atama ni shitai n' da kedo.*

Nishi: *Okyaku-sama no ogushi wa, hosokute sarasara na no de, sutorēto mo waruku nai to omoimasu kedo ne.*

Tabuchi: *Sore ga iya na no yo. Ame ga furu to, peshanko ni natchau shi. Nan da ka kodomo-ppoi kanji ga shite.*

Nishi: *Sō desu ka. Mottai-nai desu ne. Gowagowa shite iya da to ossharu okyaku-sama mo ōi no ni.*

Tabuchi: *Sō kashira. Neguse wa tsuite bosabosa ni naru shi, atama no katachi no warusa wa kukkiri dechau shi, iya da wa.*

Nishi: *Sore ja, funwari zentai ni pāma o kakemasu ka. Sō sureba, petanto naru koto wa nai deshō.*

Tabuchi: *Demo, chirichiri ni dake wa naranai yō ni shite yo.*

Nishi: *Omakase kudasai. Romanchikku ni batchiri kimete mise-masu yo. Tadashi, ato wa okyaku-sama–shidai desu kedo ne.*

☆

Tabuchi: It's autumn, so I'd like my hair to look softer, lighter, more romantic.

Nishi: Your hair is very fine and silky. It wouldn't look bad if you just left it straight, you know.

Tabuchi: That's exactly what I don't like about it. When it rains, it loses all its fluff. And besides, it makes me look like a little girl somehow…

Nishi: Really? That's a shame. Many of our customers complain about their hair being hard and stiff.

Tabuchi: Well, maybe that's okay for them. I don't like silky hair because it gets all messed up when I sleep on it. It shows the lousy shape of my head, too.

Nishi: Okay, then. How about a fluffy, all-over perm? That way it won't go flat on you.

Tabuchi: But just make sure it doesn't get all frizzy.

Nishi: Trust me. When you leave here, you'll definitely look ro-mantic. After that, it's all up to you.

ふわっと (fuwatto) G / N

Soft and light. Downy, puffy, feathery. Used to describe something that is moving or floating gently.

❏ あのふわっとした雲、まるで綿菓子みたいだね。

Ano fuwatto shita kumo, maru de wata-gashi mitai da ne.

Those fluffy clouds look just like cotton candy.

❏ あのマジック・ショーにはびっくりしたわ、横になっていた人がふわっと浮くんですもの。

Ano majikku-shō ni wa bikkuri shita wa, yoko ni natte ita hito ga fuwatto uku n' desu mono.

I was really astonished by that magic show. The man lying on his back actually floated right up into the air.

さらさら (sarasara) G / N

Smooth, dry, clean, not sticky or damp (G). Used to describe the sound or feel of light, silky hair or fabric rubbing together gently (G/N). *Sarasara* can also express the smooth feeling of water flowing in a shallow brook or the fluency of a speaker or writer (G).

❏ 今日は天気がよかったから、洗濯物がさらさらに乾いたわ。

Kyō wa tenki ga yokatta kara, sentaku-mono ga sarasara ni kawaita wa.

It was nice weather today, so the laundry that was put out to dry got good and fluffy.

❏ 飲んだ後のお茶漬けさらさら、これがうまいんだなあ。

Nonda ato no ochazuke sarasara, kore ga umai n' da nā.

After a few drinks, there is nothing nicer than the way a bowl of tea and rice slides smoothly down the throat.

❏ 小川がさらさら流れている風景なんて、もう何年も見たことがないなあ。

Ogawa ga sarasara nagarete iru fūkei nante, mō nan-nen mo mita koto ga nai nā.

It seems like years since I last saw a landscape with a gently flowing stream.

❏ 貴ノ花にサインを頼んだら、いやがらずにさらさらと書いてくれたわ。

Takanohana ni sain o tanondara, iyagarazu ni sarasara to kaite kureta wa.

When I asked the sumo wrestler Takanohana for his autograph, he dashed one off without the slightest fuss.

➥ *Chazuke* (茶漬け) refers to Japanese tea or a thin broth poured over white rice. It can be elaborate. *Tai chazuke* (鯛茶漬け) and *sake chazuke* (鮭茶漬け), for example, include pieces of sea bream and salmon, respectively. Or it can be simple with just some pickles or a little garnish scattered on top of cold, leftover rice. The usual image of *chazuke*, however, is of a plain meal that is easy to prepare. The combination of rice with tea or broth makes for easy eating, so it is a good light meal after you've had a few drinks or on other occasions. *Chazuke* is held in such high regard that it is usually sports the honorific *o*: *ochazuke*.

ぺしゃんこ／ぺちゃんこ (peshanko/pechanko) N / B

Flattened, pressed down, crushed. By extension, *peshanko* and *pechanko* can also express defeat or complete failure.

❑ 鼻ぺちゃだなんて失礼ね、私の鼻はそんなにぺちゃんこじゃないわ。

Hana-pecha da nante shitsurei ne, watashi no hana wa sonna ni pechanko ja nai wa.

My nose is flat as a pancake, you say! How insulting can you get. It's not that flat at all.

❑ きのうの会議は散々だったよ、反対派にぺしゃんこにやられちゃってね。

Kinō no kaigi wa sanzan datta yo, hantai-ha ni peshanko ni yararechatte ne.

Yesterday's meeting was terrible. I was raked over the coals by the opposition.

ごわごわ (gowagowa) N / B

Stiff, rigid. Used to describe paper, cloth, leather, etc.

❑ このシーツ、糊がききすぎてごわごわになっちゃったわ。

Kono shītsu, nori ga kikisugite gowagowa ni natchatta wa.

These sheets have too much starch. They're stiff as a board.

❑ 旅館の浴衣ってどこでもごわごわだね。

Ryokan no yukata tte doko de mo gowagowa da ne.

No matter what Japanese inn you go to, the *yukata* are as stiff as cardboard.

➥ A single-layer kimono made of cotton is called a 浴衣 *yukata* (the word *kimono* usually refers to a silk garment for everyday use or, nowadays, formal occasions). Originally made of linen and worn by samurai and the nobility as a kind of bathrobe, *yukata* dyed with simple indigo-and-white patterns later spread among the common people. Now they are popular during the hot summer months and as cool robes after hot baths, and *yukata*-clad women and children lend a colorful air to *Obon* dancing and other summer festivals. Japanese inns—*ryokan*—provide *yukata* to their guests both for sleeping and lounging. While their uniform size is convenient, the *yukata* at Japanese inns are invariably stiff and starchy.

ぼさぼさ (bosabosa) B

(1) Tussled, tangled, uncombed; used to describe not only hair but also brushes, brooms, and similar objects. (2) To sit around vacantly, not doing what needs to be done.

❏ そんなぼさぼさ頭じゃ女の子にもてない*わよ。

Sonna bosabosa-atama ja onna no ko ni motenai wa yo.

You'll never get any girlfriends with your hair looking like a haystack.

> * *Moteru*: to be popular, especially with the opposite sex.

❏ 君、ぼさぼさしていないで手伝ったらどうだ。

Kimi, bosabosa shite inai de tetsudattara dō da.

How about giving me a hand instead of sitting around like a bump on a log?

くっきり (kukkiri) G / N

Distinct, clearly visible.

❏ 見晴らしがいいわね。富士山がくっきり見えるわ。

Miharashi ga ii wa ne. Fuji-san ga kukkiri mieru wa.

What a wonderful view! You can see Mt. Fuji as plain as day.

❏ 夜になると、東京タワーがくっきりと浮かび上がってきれいだよ。

Yoru ni naru to, Tōkyō-tawā ga kukkiri to ukabiagatte kirei da yo.

Tokyo Tower is really pretty at night, the way it rises up into the air so sharp and clear.

➥ Located in Shiba Kōen, a couple of miles south of the Imperial Palace, Tokyo Tower has observation platforms as well as broadcasting antennas for several television stations. After its completion in 1958, it came to symbolize Tokyo's postwar modernization, the television age, and the 1964 Tokyo Olympics. You may have seen it destroyed more than once by prehistoric beasts in Japanese monster films of the 1960s. Modeled on the Eiffel Tower (though about 110 feet taller), Tokyo Tower is nondescript by day, but when lit up at night the tower becomes a distinctive landmark visible throughout the city.

ふんわり／ふわり (funwari/fuwari)   G / N

Gently swelling, floating, billowing. Used to describe the motion of soft, light objects floating in the air (parachutes, birds, etc.) or gently covering other objects (sheets, quilts, etc.). *Fuwatto* (the first word in this list) emphasizes the floating or rising motion, while *funwari* and *fuwari* suggest a gentler feeling. Of these latter two, *funwari* implies lighter and calmer motions.

❑ 布団を干したから、ふんわりして気持ちよくなったわよ。

Futon o hoshita kara, funwari shite kimochi yoku natta wa yo.

I hung the futons out in the sun, so now they feel nice and fluffy.

❑ 丹頂鶴がふわりと雪の中に舞い上がるのを見ていると、きれいで見飽きないよ。

Tanchō-zuru ga fuwari to yuki no naka ni maiagaru no o mite iru to, kirei de miakinai yo.

The sight of white cranes soaring up into the falling snow is so beautiful that you never grow tired of it.

❑ 美奈子さん、淡いピンクのセーターに絹のスカーフをふわりと巻いて、春らしい装いだったわ。

Minako-san, awai pinku no sētā ni kinu no sukāfu o fuwari to maite, haru-rashii yosōi datta wa.

With a silk scarf wrapped lightly around her neck and a pale pink sweater, Minako had a very springtime look.

ぺたんと (petanto)   N / B

Flat, smooth, level (N). Also used to describe the sound or action of pressing a label, sticker, or other object onto a flat surface (N). Another meaning is to flop onto the floor in a slovenly manner (N/B).

❑ 私、ハイヒールは苦手なの。いつもぺたんとした底の靴をはいているわ。

Watashi, haihīru wa nigate na no. Itsumo petan to shita soko no kutsu o haite iru wa.

I'm just no good with high heels. That's why I always wear flats.

❑ 運転の方はどうかなあ。彼の車には初心者マークがぺたんとはってあったもの。

Unten no hō wa dō ka nā. Kare no kuruma ni wa shoshin-sha–māku ga petan to hatte atta mono.

I'm not so sure about his driving. His car has a beginner's sticker plastered on it.

❏ あんまり驚いたので、ぺたんと尻もちをついちゃったわ。

Anmari odoroita no de, petan to shirimochi o tsuichatta wa.

I was so startled I fell flat on my rear end (did a pratfall).

ちりちり (chirichiri) N / B

Curly, frizzy. Used especially to describe hair, yarn, etc. that has been scorched and shriveled (N). Can also express tingling caused by extreme heat or shivering caused by cold or fear (N/B).

❏ 小さいときには、ちりちりの頭をずいぶん気にしてたのよ。

Chiisai toki ni wa, chirichiri no atama o zuibun ki ni shite 'ta no yo.

When I was small, I used to worry a lot about my frizzy hair.

❏ ちりちりと何か焦げるにおいがするけれど、大丈夫かしら。

Chirichiri to nani ka kogeru nioi ga suru keredo, daijōbu kashira.

It smells like something's gotten scorched. I wonder if everything's all right.

❏ 風呂といえば家内は熱いのが好きでしてね、肌がちりちりするようなお湯に平気で入るんですよ。

Furo to ieba kanai wa atsui no ga suki deshite ne, hada ga chirichiri suru yō na oyu ni heiki de hairu n' desu yo.

Talking about baths, my wife likes them really hot, you see. She thinks nothing of getting into a scalding tub.

➡ Japanese baths have two parts, the tub itself (called the 湯舟 *yubune*) and a washing area (洗い場 *araiba*). Whether at a private home or a public bath, proper ettiquette says you should first rinse off your body in the washing area before entering the tub, since other people will be using the same water later. Then you can relax in the tub with the hot water up to your neck, soap yourself up and rinse off again in the washing area, and then get back in the tub for a final soak. These days, most bathtubs in Japan are made of stainless steel, porcelain, plastic, or tile, but the traditional wooden baths made of cedar are still prized for their subtle aroma.

ばっちり (batchiri) G

Precise, accurate, just right. Good, well done. Used informally.

❏ 原さんはいつも頭のてっぺんからつま先までばっちり決めています*ね。

Hara-san wa itsumo atama no teppen kara tsumasaki made batchiri kimete imasu ne.

Mr. Hara is always dressed just so, from head to foot.

    * *Kimeru*: to dress properly.

❑ あんちょこがあるから、試験はばっちりよ。
Anchoko ga aru kara, shiken wa batchiri yo.
I have the answer book, so I'm gonna ace the test.

The Rush Hour

Yoshio Watanabe and Kazuhiko Tanaka work at the Shinjuku Life Insurance Company. One morning in early summer, they happen to run into each other on a commuter train.

The Rush Hour

渡辺　（電車に乗ろうとして）「あ、おはようございます、田中さん。」

田中　「おはようございます。」

　　　（ドアが閉まりかけて駅員に押される）

渡辺　「うわっ、いてててて*。」

　　　（ドアが閉まって）

渡辺　「毎日これだからいやですね。**ぎゅうぎゅう**詰めの電車で、汗を**だらだら**かきながら通勤ですから。」

田中　「まったくです。会社に着くころには**くたくた**ですよ。」

渡辺　「ワイシャツも**べとべと**になるしね。」

　　　（カップルで通勤している男女を見て）

田中　「朝から**べったり**くっついているカップルもはた迷惑†だよね。」

渡辺　「ほんと❖。いちゃいちゃ❀**べたべた**しちゃって。」

田中　「**こそこそ**話したり、**くすくす**笑ったり。まったくもう。✦」

渡辺　「**ちゃらちゃら**している女も女だけど、**でれでれ**している男も男だよ。」

田中　「**いらいら**しますよね。」

　　　（電車が大きく揺れて、カップルの顔が見える）

石田　「あっ、渡辺さんおはようございます。」

渡辺　「あれっ。石田さんじゃないですか。」

石田　「家内です。」

渡辺　「うらやましいですなあ。朝から若くてきれいな奥さんと出勤なんて。」

---

* *Itetetete*: from *itai*, "it hurts."

† *Hata-meiwaku*: annoying to others nearby.

❖ *Honto*: colloquial contraction of *hontō*.

❀ For *ichicha*: see "A Spat."

✦ *Mattaku mō*: abbreviation of something like *Mattaku mō iya ni natchau yo ne* (roughly, "I'm absolutely tired of this already").

Watanabe: *(Densha ni norō to shite) A, ohayō gozaimasu, Tanaka-san.*

Tanaka: *Ohayō gozaimasu.*

(Doa ga shimarikakete eki-in ni osareru)

Watanabe: *Uwa—, itetetete.*

(Doa ga shimatte)

Watanabe: *Mainichi kore da kara iya desu ne. Gyūgyū-zume no densha de, ase o daradara kakinagara tsūkin desu kara.*

Tanaka: *Mattaku desu. Kaisha ni tsuku koro ni wa kutakuta desu yo.*

Watanabe: *Waishatsu mo betobeto ni naru shi ne.*

(Kappuru de tsūkin shite iru danjo o mite)

Tanaka: *Asa kara bettari kuttsuite iru kappuru mo hata-meiwaku da yo ne.*

Watanabe: *Honto. Ichaicha betabeta shichatte.*

Tanaka: *Kosokoso hanashitari, kusukusu warattari. Mattaku mō.*

Watanabe: *Charachara shite iru onna mo onna da kedo, deredere shite iru otoko mo otoko da yo.*

Tanaka: *Iraira shimasu yo ne. (Densha ga ōkiku yurete, kappuru no kao ga mieru)*

Ishida: *A—, Watanabe-san ohayō gozaimasu.*

Watanabe: *Are—. Ishida-san ja nai desu ka.*

Ishida: *Kanai desu.*

Watanabe: *Urayamashii desu nā. Asa kara wakakute kirei na okusan to shukkin nante.*

☆

Watanabe: (about to board the train) Ah, Tanaka. Good morning.

Tanaka: Good morning.

Watanabe: (shoved in by a station attendant as the door closes) Yipes! Ouch ouch ouch!!!

Watanabe: (after the door has closed) This is why I hate commuting every day. Packed into a train like a bunch of sardines, we get drenched in sweat just getting to work.

Tanaka: You can say that again. By the time you get to the office, you're absolutely beat.

Watanabe: And your shirt gets all sticky, besides.

            (Here they notice a young couple.)

Tanaka: They're a real eyesore, aren't they, these young couples hanging all over each other first thing in the morning.

Watanabe: And how! They're so kissy-kissy, lovey-dovey.

Tanaka: Whispering to each other, giggling… It's just too much! (Give me a break!)

Watanabe: I don't know which is worse: the girl flirting with the guy or the guy making goo-goo eyes at the girl.

Tanaka: It's downright annoying, isn't it.

            (The train lurches, and the couple's faces come into view.)

Ishida: Ah, Watanabe. Good morning.

Watanabe: Why, if it isn't Ishida.

Ishida: And this is my wife.

Watanabe: How lucky can you be, on your way to work with such a pretty young wife…

ぎゅうぎゅう (gyūgyū) N / B

(1) To push, pull, twist, press, jam, or squeeze completely, leaving no leeway or slack. (2) To pester, harass, torment, or—as in the second example—train someone rigorously and without mercy.

❑ 太っちゃって困るわ。ジーパンのジッパー、ぎゅうぎゅう引っぱらないと上がらないのよ。

Futotchatte komaru wa. Jīpan no jippā, gyūgyū hipparanai to agaranai no yo.

My gosh, I've put on so much weight I can't get the zipper up on my jeans unless I really yank on it.

❑ 学生時代には水泳部でね、コーチにぎゅうぎゅう絞られたよ。

Gakusei-jidai ni wa suiei-bu de ne, kōchi ni gyūgyū shiborareta yo.

When I was on the swim team in college, the coach really put us through the wringer.

➤ Rush hour around Tokyo and other big Japanese cities is a wonder to behold. Nearly everyone travels by train or subway, and one-way commutes of more than an hour are typical. At the busiest times—between 7 and 9 A.M. and 6 and 8 P.M.—trains on some lines run less than two minutes apart. Nevertheless, they get so crowded that attendants at some stations have to push the overflow passengers onto the train so the doors can close. The worst times are the summer, when even air-conditioned couches get hot and sticky, and the winter, when people's bulky coats make the crush even tighter.

だらだら (daradara)　N / B

(1) The continuous dripping of sweat, blood, saliva, or another thickish liquid (N). (2) To drag on, to continue without a reasonable conclusion; to dawdle, to loaf (B). (3) Used to describe a gentle slope (N).

❏ エアロビクスを1時間もやれば、汗がだらだら流れるわよ。

Earobikusu o ichi-jikan mo yareba, ase ga daradara nagareru wa yo.

After doing aerobics for an hour, I'm simply dripping with sweat.

❏ 血がだらだら流れるような番組を見ながら、よく*ご飯が食べられるわね。

Chi ga daradara nagareru yō na bangumi o minagara, yoku gohan ga taberareru wa ne.

It's amazing how you can eat while watching such a gory program.

> * *Yoku*: ironical usage, hinting at the audacity, impertinence, or nerve shown in carrying out an action.

❏ だらだら残業をしていればいいっていうもんじゃないんだよ、君。

Daradara zangyō o shite ireba ii tte iu mon ja nai n' da yo, kimi.

Listen, my friend. Overtime is not just a matter of whiling the hours away.

❏ 郵便局の手前を右に入って、だらだらした坂を上りきるとうちなの。よかったらいらして。

Yūbin-kyoku no temae o migi ni haitte, daradara shita saka o agarikiru to uchi na no. Yokattara irashite.

If you turn right just before the post office and then go all the way up the gradual slope, there's my house. Feel free to drop by.

くたくた (kutakuta)　N / B

(1) Tired, exhausted, worn out, beat. (2) Limp, withered, collapsed, unable to maintain the proper shape.

❏ きょうは一日中引っ越しの手伝いをしたから、くたくただよ。

Kyō wa ichinichi-jū hikkoshi no tetsudai o shita kara, kutakuta da yo.

I spent all day helping someone move, so now I'm totally wiped out.

❏ おひたし*はくたくたになるまで煮ちゃだめよ。

Ohitashi wa kutakuta ni naru made nicha dame yo.

When you boil *ohitashi*, don't let it get all soft and limp.

> * *Ohitashi*: lightly boiled greens flavored with soy sauce and covered with flakes of dried bonito; typical Japanese home cooking.

べとべと (betobeto) N / B

Sticky, pasty, gluey, gummy, viscous.

❏ べとべとのガムを髪の毛にくっつけるなんて、悪質ないたずらね。

Betobeto no gamu o kami no ke ni kuttsukeru nante, akushitsu na itazura ne.

That's a pretty awful prank, putting sticky chewing gum into somebody's hair.

❏ ヘア・クリームはべとべとしているから、あんまり好きじゃないんだ。

Hea-kurīmu wa betobeto shite iru kara, anmari suki ja nai n' da.

I'm not very partial to hair oil because it's so sticky.

べったり (bettari) N / B

(1) Used to describe a sticky or adhesive object that is attached firmly to another object (N). (2) By extension, it can also refer to two people who are very close or intimate, especially when one person is overly dependent. Both meanings emphasize that the connection or relationship continues for some time (N/B).

❏ コートに泥がべったり付いているけど、一体どうしたの。

Kōto ni doro ga bettari tsuite iru kedo, ittai dō shita no.

Your coat is plastered with mud. How on earth did that happen?

❏ 大学生になっても母親べったりの息子なんて、気持ち悪いよ。

Daigaku-sei ni natte mo haha-oya–bettari no musuko nante, kimochi warui yo.

It's pretty sickening to see a guy already in college who hangs on his mother like that.

べたべた (betabeta) B

(1) Sticky, gummy. (2) Used to describe a man and woman who are overtly and immoderately affectionate. (3) For a great many pieces

of paper (posters, fliers, etc.) to be pasted on a surface, for a paper to be stamped with many seals, for a surface to be covered too thickly with paint, etc. Excess is emphasized. While *betobeto* focuses on the stickiness of an object in itself, *betabeta* emphasizes the fact that one object sticks to another. Thus *betobeto* would not be possible for meanings (2) and (3).

❑ 汗っかき*ですぐ手がべたべたするの、いやになるわ。

Asekkaki de sugu te ga betabeta suru no, iya ni naru wa.

I sweat a lot, so my hands get sticky right away. It's so annoying.

　　* *Asekkaki*: colloquial for *asekaki*, or someone who sweats a great deal.

❑ 町中であんまりカップルにべたべたされると、夏なんか暑苦しいよね。

Machinaka de anmari kappuru ni betabeta sareru to, natsu nanka atsukurushii yo ne.

When you see young couples around town hanging all over each other, summer seems even hotter than ever.

❑ うちの塀に無断でポスターをべたべたはられちゃって、はがすのに一苦労だったよ。

Uchi no hei ni mudan de posutā o betabeta hararechatte, hagasu no ni hito-kurō datta yo.

Somebody stuck a bunch of posters all over our wall without permission. It was a tough job getting them off.

こそこそ (kosokoso) B

Secretive, sneaky, furtive, sly.

❑ こそこそと人の悪口を言うなんて最低だよ。

Kosokoso to hito no warukuchi o iu nante saitei da yo.

Nothing's worse than bad-mouthing somebody behind their back.

❑ うちの子ったら、ちょっと目を離すとこそこそいたずらしているんだから困るわ。

Uchi no ko ttara, chotto me o hanasu to kosokoso itazura shite iru n' da kara komaru wa.

If I take my eyes off my son for even a second, he sneaks off and gets into some mischief. It's a real problem.

くすくす (kusukusu) N / B

To giggle or titter, especially in a suppressed voice. Usually used to describe women.

❏ どうも人がくすくす笑うと思ったら、洗濯屋の名札をつけたまま背広を着てたんだ。

Dōmo hito ga kusukusu warau to omottara, sentaku-ya no nafuda o tsuketa mama sebiro o kite 'ta n' da.

I had this feeling people were laughing behind my back, and sure enough, the suit I was wearing still had the dry cleaner's tag on it.

❏ お葬式でくすくす笑うなんて不謹慎だよ。

Osōshiki de kusukusu warau nante fu-kinshin da yo.

It's discourteous to giggle like that at a funeral.

ちゃらちゃら (charachara) N / B

(1) Rattle, jangle, clatter. The sound of small, thin metallic objects striking against each other or against something hard (N). (2) Flirtatious, coquettish, fawning. Also used to criticize the wearing of flashy, gaudy clothes. Principally used to describe women who flirt and fawn. When describing a man, the word suggests effeminacy (B).

❏ 小銭をズボンのポケットに入れておくと、ちゃらちゃらいってみっともないわよ。

Kozeni o zubon no poketto ni irete oku to, charachara itte mittomo-nai wa yo.

You're going to seem pretty silly if you put a lot of jangling coins in your pocket.

❏ 彼女ったら、ちゃらちゃらしちゃって、会社を何だと思っているのかしら。

Konojo ttara, charachara shichatte, kaisha o nan da to omotte iru no kashira.

She's really something, decked out fit to kill and playing up to (flirting with) every guy in the office. Where does she think she is, anyway?

でれでれ (deredere) B

(1) Sloppy, undisciplined, loose, slovenly. (2) *Deredere* is often used to describe a man who fawns upon a woman in a disgraceful or unbecoming manner.

❏ 道いっぱいに広がってしゃべりながらでれでれ歩いている人たちって、本当に迷惑よね。

Michi iippai ni hirogatte shaberinagara deredere aruite iru hitotachi tte, hontō ni meiwaku yo ne.

People who blithely stroll along chattering among themselves and blocking the street are really a nuisance.

❑ 女の子に囲まれるとすぐでれでれするんだから、課長も困ったもん
だよ。

*Onna no ko ni kakomareru to sugu deredere suru n' da kara, kachō mo
komatta mon da yo.*

The section chief is really a case, the way he gets all goofy-eyed whenever he's surrounded by the office girls.

いらいら (iraira) B

To become irritated, annoyed, or fidgety because things do not work
out as expected. The word may refer to one's facial expression,
actions, or manner of speaking. It is derived from the older *ira*
("thorn"). (During the Iran-Iraq War of the 1980s, some clever headline writers called it the イライラ戦争 *ira-ira sensō*, abbreviating the
names of the two countries to express irritation about that interminable conflict.)

❑ 公衆電話で長話をされるといらいらするね。

Kōshū-denwa de nagabanashi o sareru to iraira suru ne.

I get antsy if I have to wait while somebody talks for a long time on a
pay phone.

❑ 高速道路の渋滞ほどいらいらするものはないわね。

Kōsoku-dōro no jūtai hodo iraira suru mono wa nai wa ne.

Nothing sets your nerves more on edge than being caught in traffic on
the expressway.

Index

JAPANESE FOR BUSY PEOPLE
I & II

Association for Japanese-Language Teaching

This two-volume language-learning program makes it possible to communicate effectively in both business and social contexts.

I

Text: 216 pages; paperback
Tapes: four 30-minute tapes
Compact Discs: two 60-minute discs
Workbook: text: 184 pages; paperback
Workbook: tapes: two 50-minute tapes
Teachers Manual: 160 pages; paperback

II

Text: 424 pages; paperback
Tapes: six 60-minute tapes

JAPANESE-LANGUAGE
LEARNING MATERIALS

FROM KODANSHA INTERNATIONAL, LTD.

KODANSHA'S ROMANIZED JAPANESE-ENGLISH DICTIONARY

An easy-to-use, comprehensive dictionary for learners with 16,000 entries listed alphabetically, and defined for English speakers.

688 pages; Vinyl flexibinding

KODANSHA'S COMPACT KANJI GUIDE

A compact Japanese-English character dictionary based on the 1,945 Jōyō ("common use") Kanji. 20,000 practical words.

928 pages; Vinyl flexibinding

THE COMPLETE GUIDE TO EVERYDAY KANJI

Yaeko S. Habein and Gerald B. Mathias

A systematic guide to remembering and understanding the 1,945 Jōyō ("common use") *Kanji*.

344 pages; paperback

READING JAPANESE
FINANCIAL NEWSPAPERS

Association for Japanese-Language Teaching

A must for business people who need direct access to the financial pages of Japanese newspapers.

388 pages; paperback

LET'S LEARN
HIRAGANA

Yasuko Kosaka Mitamura

These workbooks explain in simple, clear steps how to read and write *hiragana* and *katakana*.

72 pages; paperback

LET'S LEARN
KATAKANA

Yasuko Kosaka Mitamura

These workbooks explain in simple, clear steps how to read and write *hiragana* and *katakana*.

88 pages; paperback

JAPANESE KANA
WORKBOOK

P. G. O'Neill

Designed to give the beginning student a systematic introduction to the *kana* and their usage.

128 pages; paperback

POWER JAPANESE SERIES

An ongoing series of compact, affordable guides dedicated to the learning and improvement of essential language skills.

Other titles in this series:

ALL ABOUT KATAKANA

Anne Matsumoto Stewart

A quick, easy way to learn *katakana* and increase your vocabulary at the same time.

144 pages; paperback

ALL ABOUT PARTICLES

Naoko Chino

Discover new particles and recall the old while learning proper usage.

128 pages; paperback

BEYOND POLITE JAPANESE

A Dictionary of Japanese Slang and Colloquialisms

Akihiko Yonekawa

Wean yourself from the textbooks. Learn to speak more like the Japanese do.

176 pages; paperback

"BODY" LANGUAGE

Jeffrey G. Garrison

Have fun learning common idioms and expressions referring to the human body.

128 pages; paperback

GONE FISHIN'
New Angles on Perennial Problems

Jay Rubin

Clears up, with intelligence and wit, the most problematic aspects of the language.

128 pages; paperback

INSTANT VOCABULARY THROUGH PREFIXES AND SUFFIXES

Timothy J. Vance

Learn hundreds of new words by modifying your existing vocabulary.

128 pages; paperback

KODANSHA NIHONGO FOLKTALES SERIES

Hiroko C. Quackenbush, Ph.D., General Editor

Momotaro, The Peach Boy
The Grateful Crane
The Runaway Riceball

A fun and easy way to practice reading comprehension of *hiragana* through traditional Japanese folktales.

All books: 32 pages; paperback